T0070171

War
before
Wisdom

War before Wisdom

BARBARA S. ANDREWS

WAR BEFORE WISDOM

Copyright © 2020 Barbara S. Andrews.

All rights reserved. No part of this book may be used or reproduced by any means, graphic, electronic, or mechanical, including photocopying, recording, taping or by any information storage retrieval system without the written permission of the author except in the case of brief quotations embodied in critical articles and reviews.

The Authorized (King James) Version of the Bible ('the KJV'), the rights in which are vested in the Crown in the United Kingdom, is reproduced here by permission of the Crown's patentee, Cambridge University Press.

iUniverse books may be ordered through booksellers or by contacting:

iUniverse
1663 Liberty Drive
Bloomington, IN 47403
www.iuniverse.com
844-349-9409

Because of the dynamic nature of the Internet, any web addresses or links contained in this book may have changed since publication and may no longer be valid. The views expressed in this work are solely those of the author and do not necessarily reflect the views of the publisher, and the publisher hereby disclaims any responsibility for them.

Any people depicted in stock imagery provided by Getty Images are models, and such images are being used for illustrative purposes only.
Certain stock imagery © Getty Images.

ISBN: 978-1-6632-0814-9 (sc)
ISBN: 978-1-6632-0813-2 (e)

Library of Congress Control Number: 2020916764

Print information available on the last page.

iUniverse rev. date: 09/25/2020

CONTENTS

ACKNOWLEDGMENTS

I would like to first thank God for the opportunity of experiencing life in the natural and spiritual. It was important to recognize that in my natural state, I experienced the humiliation of worldly injustices, but in the spirit, I was lifted from unjustifiable worldly judgments to miraculous and undeniable paradigm shifts. In my ability to yield to the indwelling spirit, God led me down an extensive road to Damascus, and along that journey, God enhanced my knowledge of him and allowed me to see myself for who I was in his eyes. The long tread was inevitably painful but well respected, as my internal bodily organs were revived and reshaped to obey God's voice.

Year after year I found myself in the valley and the wilderness, treading a lost path on my own, living a life I created to work comfortably for myself. He showed me visions of how detrimental that was to my life. God's purpose and destiny for my life had been stifled ever since my childhood. I ran into many brick walls trying to excel on my own without God. When I allowed God to reconstruct my way of thinking and redirect my steps, I understood that regardless of the circumstances of life, and the obstacles that comes with it, he would always be with me (Matthew 28:20). He proved to never leave me or forsake me (Deuteronomy 31:6). He resuscitated me and taught me how to breathe again (Genesis 2:7). He fed me his word so that my bones would be waxed strong and I would live contrary to my naturalness (Exodus 27:1-14). Thank you, Lord, for your divine order!

I am grateful for the family that helped me to escape the madness that I helplessly experienced during my childhood. I would also like to thank the couple from Jamaica who was filled with the true spirit of God, mentored me, and showed me how to allow God to resuscitate me from human death to spiritual life. Thank you for embracing me and welcoming me into your family. I also want to thank their family for embracing me and adopting me and my children as their family.

I would like to thank everyone who shared a romantic relationship with me and marriage. I know they did not go well as planned, but they have helped me in many ways. Thank you for allowing me to lean on you while struggling with my past experiences, trust that I appreciated your love, acceptance, and your willing efforts to battle with me, even when I didn't understand my life. I pray that your lives are that much more accomplished and filled with the joy of the Lord.

I would like to thank my parents, my children, siblings, spiritual leaders, friends, and associates for all the prayers, affirmations, and experiences and for the precious moments of battle that led us to the next level of rebuilding and reshaping our relationships. God designed those life mishaps to open our hearts and minds to divine intervention, manipulated so we will be led—by him and for him— toward a foundation of unity. I can smile today because all of you played a part in getting me over being bound by my past. I love you all!

INTRODUCTION

The book began with a love story, continued to moments of brokenness, and ends with a restored life with the love of God and relationship. The story is about a little girl who faced many life challenges that caused her to make bad decisions. Not really understanding life, as there were always dysfunctional behaviors around her, she sought ways to escape but had a hard time doing it. It appeared that everyone was corrupt and had some form of dysfunction that denied her the help she needed from them. A friend led her to God, whom she allowed to lead her down the road to Damascus (a journey of meeting God), where she experienced war along the way but gained wisdom in the end. The world has dealt a bad hand to many people who have not had the opportunity to choose their paths in life. When they finally got away, they exemplified the behaviors they had seen and coupled it with diverse ways to resolve them on their own. They too got caught in the war of the world and needed godly wisdom to bail them out.

My goal with *War before Wisdom* is to help those who have experienced a hard life growing up, regardless of what it was, how it happened, or what caused it. I hope to inspire them to press forward without giving up. The important thing for them to understand is though war rage in their bodies it is typical humanity; it is designed to deter them from the wisdom of God. The wisdom of humanity is limited without God, as it has its own way of living life that contradicts God's principles of life. Humanity often sees God as an imaginary spirit that people conjure up. If they give God the opportunity, he would prove to them he is not a fairy tale. This book addresses how God changed Sheaba's life when she accepted him, believed in him, and trusted him with her life. He allowed her to see things a bit deeper than she could ever have imagined on her own. Sheaba's life will encourage others to have hope in knowing that life does not end with a sad story, and they too can have an opportunity to live a happy life as God planned.

As you soon will see, Sheaba battled more than half of her life, trying to understand life and what it meant for her. She searched in places that created excruciating pain and suffering, so much so that she became numb to it. If God had allowed her to live, then why wouldn't she yield to his teachings? It would only teach her, through his word, how to search herself and make valid steps to change? While learning the word of God, Sheaba recognized that majority of the time, she inflicted self-hurt, which eventually built storms in her life. The storms in her life hurled in like a Tsunami until she accepted a shift in her mind through Christ.

When a tsunami hits someone's life, suicide is often the next step, and if there is no trust in God, it will win. Through God, life can be seen for what it is—preventing physical death from the storms it brings. First Corinthians 10:13 says, "No temptation has overtaken you that is not common to man. God is faithful and he will not let you be tempted beyond your ability but with temptation he will also provide the way of escape, that you may be able to endure it" (ESV). Many, like Sheaba, have attempted suicide multiple times, but God never allowed it to be fulfilled. Though your hearts and minds may be filled with indignation and may have fulfilled the lusts of your flesh, God is standing by to meet you where you are.

I believe anyone who reads this book will relate to Sheaba's many encounters and will, at times, smile, laugh, cry, and gain strength. I have put my heart and soul into giving readers the big picture of what it is to grow up angry, without true love, and faced with afflictions and a lack of wisdom, and to eventually gain wisdom and learn how to live life with understanding. It is my hope that this book starts the beginning of a healing process to those who are experiencing life's mishaps that stimulated identity crisis, low self-esteem, resentment, anger, and the like. Also, to those who may have not experienced tough life jilting situations, understand that no one is exempt from the struggles of life, and you too can learn from Sheaba's life. Everyone can have hope in knowing that although they have experienced difficult life-changing events, going through them will be worthwhile. There are people who truly care; they are those people who stick closer to you than your own family (Proverbs 18:24) and have been blessed with the strength of God to journey with you through your struggles.

Inspired by my own writing, telling Sheaba's story healed me from my past. I had forgiven many and was able to discuss painful areas of my life without feeling bitter. With the help of God, I learned myself, and how my life was solely based on worldly perceptions. He alone gave me the strength to stand up, face my giants, and love them with Godly love (Matthew 5:44). While writing this book, I cried, I smiled, and I got angry, but I fought through it and accepted that without God, life can be a living hell when you don't understand it or have someone to guide you through it in truth.

To this day I have a strong relationship with God; I recognized all that I went through was uprooted, washed, delivered, and purged from my soul. Writing Sheaba's story gave me hope, and I believe it will do the same for my readers. I hope you will be able to forgive others as well as yourselves. Also, I hope you can redirect your thoughts, and any evil actions or words that stems from your heart when you are backed into a corner. The storms may be raging around about, but if you try to stand unmovable in the faith of God, you might be surprised to experience a win in your life, even when it feels like you are losing.

It is important to get out of the old and step into the new, as this life is not promised to anyone. It is time to live a full life of joy while the grace of God abounds on earth. Don't walk one more day in guilt, shame, anger, bitterness, or any other negative emotion, which are designed to lead to a life of misery and, later, death.

—Barbara S. Andrews

CHAPTER 1

Shaped by Her Past

Sheaba's First Love Experience

Oh, how Sheaba loved him. She adored him. He was her first love, the one who would never bring harm to her. She was his queen, and he was her king; She dared someone to say he had done anything wrong. Even if the facts were clear, it did not fit her king. Whenever she needed comfort, he was there to sing to her and tell her how beautiful she was. He stroked her ego and built up her self-esteem. She was special, and he considered her his first lady, his princess. Whenever she looked in his eyes, goose pimples covered her body. In her vulnerability and innocence, she succumbed to his every word and action. His vision was her vision, and his instructions enforced her obedience.

What a mighty man, she thought. He was vigorous and tall, his intellect was clear, and his tone was deep. His hands were large; and when he held her hand it gave off an overwhelming security. When he held her near, the warmth of his body caused her heart to beat rapidly, and instantly caused her to relax. The kind of love they shared made it impossible for them to separate. He was the epitome of genuine love. And that is where it all began.

One day, Sheaba woke up and looked for her first love. Where was he? Where was the music of his fingers snapping, hands clapping, and singing in the shower? The silence caused an unknown fear that forced her to quickly climb out of bed and scurry down the hall to look for him. Her little feet pitter-pattered down the hall. Her heart was filled with disappointment when she saw him standing in the living room with another woman. Heartbroken, she stood listening to their conversation but could not understand what they were saying. She stood in the hall, waiting to be acknowledged.

The woman looked in Sheaba's direction, which caused her first love to look as well. He smiled at her and said, "I will be with you shortly, go back to your room." Stunned, she stood stiff with her mouth glued shut and her legs trembling. Her eyes filled with tears, and pain traveled quickly throughout her body. He walked over to Sheaba, gently took her hand, and walked her to her bedroom. He stooped down in front of her and wiped her tears. He spoke words of encouragement and affirmation to comfort her, as he always did. His presence, touch, and the sound of his voice never failed to win her over. As she calmed herself, he talked her into finding something to do while he finished his business with the woman. Trusting him was easy, as he had never lied to her about anything.

So she waited patiently for his return. A moment later, Sheaba heard music playing, which was usually her cue to join him. She quickly ran out of the room and leaped into his arms. He laughed loudly, lifted her with his strong arms, kissed her cheeks, and then placed her on the floor. They danced and sang and enjoyed their time together until she got tired. The woman never left, but she was out of sight. Sheaba didn't care; she was so happy to be with her first love that she tuned out the thoughts of the woman.

Months went by, and Sheaba and her first love continued with their daily dancing and singing as the music played loud daily in their Livingroom. Suddenly, the woman that Sheaba seen in their house from time to time appeared again. Bewildered, Sheaba battled to make sense out of what was going on. Although she did not quite understand what she was feeling and why she felt the way she did toward the woman, she knew she did not like it. Who was this woman, and why was she there? Her small mind could barely understand her own existence, and her emotions were too much to handle. She had no idea that as she got older, those emotions would shape her future. The more she thought of the woman being with her first love, the more distant she became. The change in her behavior sparked her first love's concern. He didn't like her being sad; he always found a way to make his princess happy. He made time to talk with her to find out what was going on, but before she could answer, the woman approached them.

Sheaba lifted her eyes to look at the woman and tears streamed from her eyes and down her cheeks. Immediately, he embraced her and said, "everything is okay. Remember I will always be here for you." Sheaba held on to him tightly and buried her face into his chest, wetting his shirt with her tears. The woman sat down next to them, and Sheaba heard her say, "It is time to make some changes."

Before he agreed, he took his index finger and lifted Sheaba's chin from his chest, gazed into her eyes, and said softly, "Daddy is not going anywhere, but you have to spend more time with your mother. There are many things that she must show that are helpful to your growth from a growing little girl to a young lady."

Sheaba lifted her eyes to investigate her father's, surprised that the woman she was jealous of was her mother. She nodded in agreement but not before he promised that they would never stop having their time together.

Sheaba was Daddy's little girl; she was spoiled, and it seemed to her that it was only them. Her mother, Thelma, recognized the need to separate the two, as it would become a problem in the future with her siblings. Oh yes, Sheaba had five brothers, whom she had also blocked out of her mind. Although her selfish acts were innocent, they had to be squashed before things got more complicated. Slowly, Thelma broke the strong grip of Sheaba and her dad, Bobby. It was hard at first, as Sheaba was accustomed to the things she and Bobby would do daily.

Sheaba cried and threw tantrums, because being with Thelma was not the same as being with her first love. Eventually, Thelma succeeded in separating Sheaba from her daily rituals with her dad.

Thelma found ways to capture Sheaba's attention with reading books and other activities in which Sheaba was interested. She took Sheaba shopping and bought her a couple of dolls and a kitchen set, and whenever Thelma would cook, she allowed Sheaba to be right there to help. After a while, Sheaba learned to balance her time with both of her parents, which made it easier for them to focus on all the children without jealousy.

It was a mother's love that quickly broke the chain of selfishness, which later might have hindered her development. As Sheaba became more accustomed to the changes, her selfish eyes were opened to her siblings, and she began interacting with them as well. Now that things were in perspective, Thelma and Bobby had more time with each other without drama. Sheaba did not have a total change of heart; she still looked forward to being with her dad more than anyone else.

When Sheaba was born, Bobby held her in his arms, and when she opened her eyes for the first time, she saw him, and when he spoke, his voice resonated in her heart. He spent a lot of time with her, as Thelma had her hands full with the three older boys. Thelma birthed two more boys after Sheaba, neither of whom took her place with Bobby, which was why she developed that strong selfish bond with him.

Sheaba was so caught up in enjoying her life with the changes that she did not realize that her first love was slipping away. Bobby and Thelma had been going through a rough patch for a long time. For a little while, they were discreet about it, and then things got so bad that their quarrels were obvious. Sheaba noticed her mom would be in one area of the house, and her dad would be in another.

Sheaba went to her dad, as she no longer saw the joy in his eyes, and it saddened her. Bobby lifted her onto his lap.

"Are you okay?" she asked, smiling.

He returned the smile but said sadly, "Some things you will never understand, but I want you to know that no matter what, Daddy loves his little princess." Before Sheaba knew it, her first love disappeared from her life. Thelma appeared stressed and was always busy doing something around the house. Everything changed at home without

4

her dad. There was no loud music, thunderous laughter, or excitement. Things became more structured—Thelma instructed everyone to take routine naps. Breakfast, lunch, and dinner where scheduled at the same time every day, A bath and bedtime were always a few hours after dinner. Thelma read to them and tucked them into bed, but Sheaba longed for the touch of her dad, her first love.

Though Sheaba did not stop thinking of her dad, she learned a lot about her mother, and she treasured their time together. Thelma was beautiful; she stood about five feet tall and had smooth chocolate-brown skin. Her hair was long, black, and thick; at times she wore it in a ponytail. She often dressed up to go out with her friends or on a date, and Sheaba was usually there to watch. The costly jewels and array with which her mother adorned herself was fascinating. Thelma's dresser was filled with perfumes, jewelry, and other things to her liking. In the closet, her clothes hung neatly and looked to be expensive. As Thelma got herself dressed, Sheaba looked at her in amazement—she looked like a different person. Thelma smiled at Sheaba and dabbed a little bit of perfume on her and quickly painted her nails. Before leaving, she would always make sure everyone was fed, bathed, and in the bed, sound asleep. When they woke up, she would be home, as if she had never left.

One morning, Sheaba woke up sobbing, and Thelma quickly made her way to her room and asked, "what is going on babe? Why the heavy tears?" Sheaba said, "I miss my daddy! Where is he mommy? Where did he go?"

For a minute, Thelma sat speechless, holding Sheaba and rocking her, trying to find the right words. "Daddy had to go away for a while. I am not sure when he will be back, but I will make sure he knows you are thinking of him."

Sheaba was confused, as she did not know what to make of that statement. Thelma grabbed Sheaba by the hand and took her to the living room, where she pulled out a few photo albums. She showed her many family photos that put a smile on her face. Each photo had a story that Thelma told. It eased Sheaba's mind and comforted her.

Thelma left Sheaba sitting on the couch with the photo albums, and her older brothers joined her.

Later that afternoon, Thelma did something a little different than she did normally. She prepared lunch and then took everyone to the park across the street from the house. She allowed them to run until they got tired; then she summoned them to come inside, washed them, and laid them down for a nap.

Thelma must have contacted Bobby while the children were napping because when Sheaba woke up, she heard his voice. The boys were already awake and with him. Sheaba screamed, *"Daddy!"* She leaped onto his lap with joy and hugged him tight. He kissed her on the cheek and said, "I love you and I miss you too my little Princess. I told you I would come back."

"Are you home to stay?" she asked.

The look in his eyes gave away the answer. He could not lie to his baby girl, so he responded with a story that brought a bit of sadness, but she had grown up since the last time they had together and was old enough to understand that his decision was for the best. "I promise I will never leave you for an extended time, and I will always make a way for us to spend time together."

Again, she trusted him, as he always found ways to put a smile on her face, which also helped him deal with the pain of walking away from her. His little girl's happiness was everything to him, but he was unable to keep his promise, which later caused Sheaba's resentment toward him.

That day when Sheaba saw her dad was the last time for a while. She wondered what had happened to him—he told her he would never leave for a long time without finding a way to see her. Feeling deeply saddened and rejected, she stopped playing much with her siblings and drifted off to herself.

Her brothers—Howard, Duane, John, Robert, and Wesley—always found things to do to keep their minds occupied, and they had each other, but Sheaba was alone. John and Sheaba were close in age, and they would sometimes hang out together. He would notice her sitting alone looking sad and ask, "Would you like to play our favorite game "house" with the dolls and the dishes or what would you like to do? Sheaba smiled as she always did and said, "Yes! Yes! Let's do it!" John did not bother to ask what was wrong, he just wanted to make her feel like she belonged. Their mom was always busy, and Sheaba was the only girl in the family, so John tried to provide Sheaba with a little fun. Robert and Wesley were still very young and were with Thelma the majority of the time.

The atmosphere in the household shifted again, and everyone did whatever they needed to do to remain happy. Thelma continued with her daily routine—and then one day, Sheaba saw her mom with a new man. Sheaba was not happy about that, but she had no power to change what was happening. One evening, Sheaba was sitting on the floor of the living room, watching television. Thelma and the man were sitting on the couch behind her. Sheaba turned around to tell her mom she needed to go to the bathroom and caught the two locking lips.

"Why are you kissing that man?" Sheaba cried. "And where is my dad?"

"Turn around and watch TV," Thelma yelled.

Sheaba complied, but she began crying and wet herself.

"Maybe I've come around too soon," the man whispered.

"Sheaba's too young to understand what's going on," Thelma said.

Angry, Sheaba sat in her mess and waited for her mom's company to leave. After Thelma walked the man to the door, she called for Sheaba. "Sheaba! Sheaba! Come here!" Sheaba was afraid to move, so she sat silently.

Thelma walked back to the living room. "Did you hear me calling you little girl?" she asked.

Sheaba nodded her head but still did not move.

Thelma quickly recognized why she would not move. She picked Sheaba up and spanked her bottom. "You wet yourself for attention!" Thelma snapped. And her next hurtful words saddened Sheaba's heart: "Your dad is not coming back, so get over it!"

Now that Sheaba knew her dad was never coming back, she leaned on her brothers for the comfort her dad would have given. It was totally different, but it kept her mind at peace for a while. The boys began to open themselves to her in a way that was not conducive to her female continuity. They embraced her as their own gender, imposing upon her their masculinity. Sheaba fell right into place, she did not have a choice but to receive what they imposed. She took on their male traits and became solid as a rock in strength. There was no fear in her when it came time to standing up against anyone physically. Regrettably, she had no sister to balance the toughness she had gained from her siblings. Playtime was always with the boys and oftentimes their friends. Nevertheless, she was happy with having the power of both worlds, male and female, but eventually, it imposed a disrespect to her gender. The fact that Sheaba emerged into male dominance, it caused her to be handled roughly, dismissing her girlish frame into one that exemplified a tomboy. Sheaba had no idea the tomboyish ways, along with her father's absence, and the rejection she felt from it, would reshape her worth, integrity, character, mentality, and her ability to have healthy relationships.

Sheaba was smart and had been very self-confident until she began experiencing a plethora of life-changing events in her household that caused discomfort and a broken heart.

All Grown Up with Aggression

Sheaba was tall, with a caramel complexion and medium-length thick black hair. She was very skinny and had undefined curves. She was still Daddy's little girl. In his absence, her heart longed for him but not as much as before. Although she was a few years from becoming a pre-teen it felt as if life had forced her into a game of Russian roulette. She viewed life that way because of her dysfunctional household, which caused her great confusion.

After a few years had passed, Bobby came back to visit. Thelma opened the door and said, "Well what a surprise! What blows you by?" Bobby said, "Don't start no mess Thelma. I just came by to let you know I live in the complex across the street. Please allow me to take the kids to my place." Thelma was not enthusiastic about it, but Sheaba was ecstatic. Even though her feelings for her dad were not as strong as they once had been, she was glad to see him. With Bobby nearby, she had high hopes that they could rekindle their relationship. Thelma said, "fine, just don't take them too far without letting me know where they are going. I hope you don't mess that up like you did everything else." Bobby ignored Thelma's comment and said, "Are the boys around? If so, please get them ready." Thelma responded, "The boys can go next time. They are outside playing and I am not going to go looking for them. Go ahead and take Sheaba." Sheaba, overly excited, literally tried rushing her mother to get her ready. "Relax Sheaba! "Sorry mom!" said Sheaba. "I need you to be on your best behavior. Ok Sheaba?" Sheaba said, "Yes ma'am!" "Your dad will be introducing you to his new lady and her children." said Thelma. "O.K momma," said Sheaba. Bobby and Sheaba walked out of the house hand in hand smiling at each other. When they got inside of Bobby's new home, Sheaba noticed the woman her dad was dating looked a lot older than her mom, and her children were already of age. Sheaba thought, "well at least I have a big sister, someone to have girly time with and do girly things." The visit went well. Everyone appeared to be nice and cordial. Sheaba and her new sister, Darlene, got along well, but jealousy set in when Sheaba thought about sharing her dad with Darlene. *Would she be the center of her dad's attention?* she thought. Shortly after that first visit, Bobby and his new family moved away without leaving a forwarding address, and Bobby was out of touch again for a very long time.

Sheaba and her mom's relationship had grown tremendously. They were always together whenever she had the opportunity. They watched television, cooked, and cleaned together, and at times, her mom let her lie in her bed to nap instead of being in the room with her siblings. Being with her brothers was cool at times, but they were always rough and she had days that she just wanted to be like her mom; a lady. Anyway, her brothers did not always want her around but, that eventually changed. When Sheaba did not want to be under her mom, she wanted to be outside, but if her brothers were out already, Thelma would make her stay inside. Staying in the house was boring, but who would she play with if she went outside alone? There were no one visibly around to play with. *Maybe the girls in the neighborhood mostly stayed inside and played with their dolls and things.* Sheaba thought. Sheaba did not know any of the girls in her neighborhood, except for those at the neighborhood school. But none of them were friends outside of school. Besides, Thelma would not have allowed her to play on any porch other than her own. At times Sheaba would sit on the porch and watch her brothers play. Other times, they'd be out of view from the porch, and she was not allowed to leave the porch without permission. It was tough sitting there as they had all the fun, but she lived with it.

One bright, sunny morning, everyone was looking forward to getting outside, but Thelma refused to let anyone go out. The children were confused but followed orders. It was never safe to question their mom; that was considered disrespectful. The atmosphere was a bit different that day. Sheaba felt tension and anxiety, and Thelma appeared to be a bit on edge. Sheaba and her siblings kept their distance from her and remained silent. It was obvious that something was seriously wrong, as she paced the floor and looked out of the window from time to time.

Watching her mother's every move, Sheaba saw Thelma walk frantically to the door. Sheaba leaped up from the floor to follow. Seconds later—and before Sheaba reached the door—she heard three gunshots. Sheaba froze at the sound at first and then sprinted the rest of the way to the door, only to find her mom on the hallway floor, bleeding. Sheaba screamed at the top of her lungs. Their neighbor, Mrs. Bailey, had come out of her apartment, called 911 and forced Sheaba back into the house. Sheaba being stubborn tried to force her way to the hallway floor where her mom laid, but Mrs. Bailey held her tightly against her body and promised that she would take care of her mom. Sheaba immediately felt sick; she could feel the blood rush to her head, which made her dizzy. Her oldest brother took her hand

and led her back into the house. Anger overtook her in a way that she had never felt before; aggression married her that day. Thoughts of retaliation were comforting and scary at the same time. Violence was not in her character; love was her mission, but the moment she saw her mom on that hallway floor bleeding, she wanted to take revenge for her mom's sake.

The ambulance arrived, and Sheaba watched through the window as they carried her mom away. Mrs. Bailey walked into the apartment where Sheaba and her siblings were and said, "I have some food for you all if you get hungry. Just come and knock on my door. Now lock the doors behind me. Do not answer for anyone. I will come and check on you from time to time." "Thank you, Mrs. Bailey," said Howard, the eldest sibling.

Sheaba and her brothers were home alone for a few weeks before anyone showed up to help. Mrs. Bailey checked in on them from time to time as she promised, but she was old and sickly herself, so she eventually stopped coming by. A few family and friends brought food, but it lasted only for a little while. No one checked on them after that, so they did the best they could with what was left in the pantry. Eventually, the cupboards were bare, and the pantry was empty. That was when Howard suggested they go to the neighborhood grocery store and get something. No one was willing to go because they knew no one had money to pay for what they needed. Sheaba said, "I will go with you!" Howard said, "ok sis, but do what I tell you to do." "OK!" said Sheaba. Sheaba knew what they were about to do, and was ready to stand by her brother's side to help him do whatever needed to be done.

They were fearful, but they were also hungry; besides, the two youngest siblings could not go hungry as long as the older ones. Howard knew that if they were caught stealing, they would go to jail, and the others would be placed in the custody of Child Protective Services. Fortunately, they pulled it off with no hassle. Sheaba thanked God they did not have to do it again, as Bobby had finally come to pick them up. Unfortunately, Sheaba and her siblings' lives were not the same after that. What they thought was a good thing turned out to be bad.

The Unimaginable Shift

Bobby wasted no time making his move. That day, Sheaba and her siblings had no idea that they would never return to their mom. Immediately, Bobby reached out to social services for benefits. Shortly thereafter, they had come to the home. Prior to their arrival, Bobby forced Sheaba and her siblings to lie to the social workers about their mother's treatment toward them. He scared them so much, that those lies helped him gain custody without a fight. *Who had this man I loved so dearly become?* she thought. While Thelma was in the hospital, fighting for her life, Bobby was exercising betrayal. Sheaba loved her dad and was happy to see him at first, but when he pulled that evil stunt, she knew she could not trust him. When Thelma was released from the hospital, she searched for her children, asking many people if they knew their whereabouts; she was unsuccessful. She wept for weeks, as she had no idea where to look for them.

Bobby had no compassion for Thelma and gloated about her pain. He threatened the children so they would keep silent, and he demanded they have no contact with her. Thelma had no recollection of anything after the shooting. When she reached out to the authorities and social services, she was not able to get any leads on the whereabouts of her children. Eventually, she stopped searching, used that time to get her life in order and hoped that by then the children would be returned. Thelma had been to jail on more than one occasion due to her efforts to make money to provide for her children. Being a single mom raising six children alone in those days was tough, even with a job, so she did what she could to make ends meet.

Now Sheaba felt the same pain as when she had been apart from her dad, but this time it was for her mom. She did not understand why life was a tug-of-war. She did not know what had gone on between her mom and dad, but it looked like a lot of deception was going on. *Why are they fighting each other?* Sheaba thought. Now more mature, Sheaba again asked herself questions—but this time about both her parents. *Why did he do that? Where is Mom? Did she live through the gunshot wound?* Word reached them that she was okay and was out of the hospital.

Everything in Sheaba's mind went blank after that; nothing else was said or done. Mom was gone, and Bobby retained custody. The new environment was not comfortable, and Bobby did not help his children feel welcomed or loved. At least when they had been with their mom, only the people on the outside were against them. With their dad, it seemed as if the household and everyone on the outside were against them. Her siblings did not seem to think much of it; at least they did not appear as uncomfortable as she was. She trusted her brothers, so she followed their lead in accepting what had taken place in their lives

Shortly after Bobby moved Sheaba and her siblings into their new home, John and Sheaba were sent to their grandmother's to live. Surprisingly, Bobby suggested it. Now, that was a very happy time for them. During the week, they had the same routine at Grandma's as they always did—homework first, a little time outside riding bikes, baths, dinner, and preparation for bed. Grandma did not allow them to watch TV, so they sometimes went next door to their aunt's house. Still, Grandma did not allow them to go too often, and when she did, they could stay no more than an hour or so, as bedtime was at eight o'clock ritually. On the weekends, she taught them how to work for the things they needed. She made sure their chores were consistently done every Saturday and was paid every Sunday morning before they went to church. They enjoyed their time with Grandma, but things became a bit tough for her, and after a year, she had to send them back to Bobby. Bobby was no help to her in providing, she did everything on her own; but, he always had his hand out asking her for something.

Their experience with her was rewarding. Every weekend Grandma sent for them to work until Bobby stopped it altogether. It almost seemed as if their happiness was frowned upon. Bobby seemed to sabotage whatever kept Sheaba and her siblings functioning and at peace.

Sheaba wished she were still with her mom. It did not feel like home with her dad; too many people were in the house, and there was always something going on. Bobby never paid attention to any of his biological children, but he made himself available to Grace's children and everyone else in her family. *"Why would dad take us from mom and choose to keep us away from our mom if we're such a burden?"* she thought. Grace's eldest boy, Walter, would always ridicule and antagonize Sheaba's brothers. His sister, Darlene, played promiscuous games with Sheaba at night—and so did Walter, but majority during the day time. He was clever in his approach. He found ways to manipulate her into going to a quiet place with him, as if he were a big brother who wanted to teach her something. Sadly, it happened so often that she prepared herself for both step sibling's actions.

Walter and Darlene's "games" were not Sheaba's first experience. A couple years before Bobby took Sheaba and her siblings, the son of Thelma's best friend, who was 16 years old at the time, was babysitting them, and he tried forcing himself inside her. She was only eight years old, and it was very painful. Because she was scared, she never uttered a word of it. He had not been mean or forceful; he manipulated her by being kind. He somehow got her siblings to trust him, and they did not come looking for her, nor did they suspect anything was going on.

Likewise, the older children in their dad's home did things that forced her to enjoy those promiscuous feelings she had never experienced before because it happened consistently against her will. While it was creepy at first, she began to desire it. They opened a brand-new emotion in Sheaba that at an early age was detrimental to her future. She wasn't yet old enough to have adult desires, she was 10 years old; but those desires for their touch would arise with no actual thought or action to spark them. That alone freaked her out. Sheaba thought, *I do not want to like this feeling, but I do. I do not want to be touched by them, but it happens! I did not ask for what was done to me. Why did it happen, and who can I tell?* Unfortunately, she did not feel comfortable telling anyone. She was sure they would make her feel bad by calling her a liar or saying it was her fault. So she accepted what was being done to her. It was wrong, but her body began to long for it.

After a while, Sheaba's step siblings left her alone, and those lustful feelings subsided. Walter, however, continued taunting her siblings. He laughed at the way they dressed and simply said things to hurt their feelings. No one would come to their aid; instead, they would join in the laughter with Walter and chime in on the mockery. Consequently, the consistent verbal bashing raised Sheaba's aggression to an all-time high. This was in addition to the aggression she felt when her mother was shot and the aggression against Bobby for having no compassion for her mom.

If this is all the world has to offer—envy, bitterness, manipulation, and all other negativity—then what is the purpose to life? Sheaba thought. Sadly, Bobby, Sheaba's first love, the one she trusted and thought could do no wrong, was just as devilish as the people with whom he surrounded himself. He showed no regard for his children's safety, which proved he clearly had no love for them. He also made hurtful comments along with Walter, rather than protecting them. Sheaba and her siblings had no ground to stand on; they were unstable and outnumbered. Whenever anyone in Bobby's new family said his children did something wrong, he would believe them over his children. He would whip them at the drop of a hat and enjoy doing it. The sound of the belt hitting her brothers' skin caused Sheaba to have anxiety. Fear forced her to cry as if she was being whipped. Sheaba screamed in her thoughts, *Who is this man?*

The people to whom Bobby exposed his children were like the neighborhood they lived in—violent by nature and showing no remorse for the things they did and whoever they did them to. Although Sheaba and her brothers tried to fight for their integrity and worth, both inside and outside of their home, it was a struggle. Before Sheaba and her siblings could learn of themselves, they were torn down by their dad and his new family, just as the outside world was doing.

On the outside, Sheaba and her brothers were outcasts, as they had been in the past with their mom because they looked different. They loved playing and fighting among themselves and were not ashamed of their hand-me-down clothes. They only wanted to make friends and be cordial with the people on the outside, but all people wanted to do is scar them with negativity. Sheaba and her siblings had done a lot of running from their bullies in the past, but they soon realized that if they continued to run, they would always be bullied. Yet even when her brothers started fighting back, people kept coming at them—until they won. Not very much respect was gained from it, though. People continued to talk about Sheaba and her siblings, but they ignored them until they brought a fight to them. Sheaba and her siblings may have won those fights, but they were still fighting for respect. At least with mom, there was love applied with discipline, however, with dad, it was a lose/lose situation inside and outside of their home for a long time. Sheaba hated when anybody tried to hurt her brothers, especially the younger ones. They were never allowed to fight their own battles when Sheaba was around; she would always jump in it. They taught her well, and she was ready to exert herself at any time, but they would sometimes find ways to keep her out of their battles.

Sheaba's appearance was not that of a physically strong girl. Barely standing five feet tall, weighing only ninety pounds, she could take a blow from her brothers and strike back. She showed no fear, and she went at a battle full throttle, prepared to win. Unknowingly, aggression had become her motivation. If her back was pushed against the wall, she would come off swinging and pounding on anyone in her way. Climbing trees was her biggest interest; she wanted to see how high she could go. Not too high though, she was afraid of being too high. Climbing fences and jumping over them was her second interest. Oftentimes she would rip her pants or get a cut, but she would keep going. Even though Sheaba loved jumping rope, playing with dolls, and doing other girly things, her passion was sports. Most of all she loved fighting. Now, Sheaba would not start the fight, but she would end with a win.

When Bobby moved Sheaba and her siblings to the new neighborhood, there, Sheaba had her first fist fight. A young boy and his sister decided they wanted to break up her game of catch with her two younger brothers. She fought both on the playground in front of the house and won—no one was going to ever bully her or her younger brothers. Sheaba had also gotten into a fight with a boy when she and her older brother John lived with their grandmother. The boy was defeated, as Sheaba fought with confidence from one end of the block to the next. The boy bit her on the neck, which ultimately ended the fight. Fighting was all Sheaba had known to do, as no one respected her or her siblings unless it happened.

Bobby knew that Sheaba was a bit of a tomboy, but he still refused to let her outside alone. He would always make sure at least one of her brothers went out with her as well. Sheaba thought, *I do not understand why he do that*—and *why did he not go outside with us?* Bobby spent more time laughing at Sheaba and her siblings with Walter than being there for them. Walter never gave her brothers the benefit of the doubt. He always laughed and talked about how weak they were. Instead of Bobby taking the side of his sons, he agreed. Sheaba thought, *If they were so weak, then why would he send them out in such a violent neighborhood without accompanying them?* The fact that he rarely had been around his children, was clearly the reason he didn't understand their abilities. Dad was so rough with Sheaba and her four oldest brothers when he and mom were together. Sheaba thought, *Shoot! He was the man who instilled hostility into them through imposing his immature aggression. Why would he think they would not grow up to be fighters?*

When they were much younger, mom made them stop running from a fight and made them fight back; she threatened if they did not win, they were getting a whooping from her as well. However, dad made them fight each other, causing them to have a competitive spirit toward one another. Gratefully, Sheaba and her brothers did not allow their internal aggression toward one another to show outside of the home. It took nothing for them to battle for each other on the outside, as they loved each other. They leaned on each other often, as they felt that no one was on their side, and it was them against the world.

Bobby never ceased attacking his children, verbally and physically. The beatings went from a belt to his fist and/or objects. Nothing they did was ever good enough, but when they finally developed certain interests, he pushed them hard to excel so that they eventually disliked it. He never supported their talents; he degraded them; He did nothing for them; it was all for himself. If he did not look good in whatever he was attempting to teach them, then he would talk down to them. He always had to get the glory for the talents of Sheaba and her siblings. He may have inadvertently inspired it but was not the leader that drove them to succeed in it. As selfish as he was, he always wanted his children to look out for him when Grace's family ganged up on him. When he did not get the support from Sheaba and her siblings, he would beat them in his frustration and anger.

Sheaba's older brothers realized the abuse had gone on long enough. They started standing up for themselves. Duane, the second born, began fighting back first, and then the eldest, Howard. Duane was hot tempered and was more apt to fight, even if he knew he would not win; he had no fear. Howard was quiet and kept busy with work and other things to keep a positive mind. The third son, John, found things to do at the neighborhood center or found ways to spend time with their grandma so he could be away from home. Duane was fed up and it showed. His aggression caused him to become a part of a dangerous group of people from the streets. This group helped him to build the courage to stand up to Bobby and Walter. Boy! Did he leave a memory for those two! Let's just say he did not leave without swinging. Howard and John left one year behind each other, but they did not leave without a fight. Sheaba was happy for her older siblings, as they each left home and never returned, allowing them to break free from the madness and find happiness in their lives. They found Thelma, who had moved to Birmingham, Alabama. She was living a better life and was in a relationship with a great man, who helped take care of her teenage boys when they arrived.

After Sheaba's older brothers left, she took on the role as the eldest at fourteen years old. Robert was twelve and Wesley was eleven, and they looked to her for everything. Sheaba did not know how to be a mother, which is what they needed, but she did her best to protect them and guide them. Sheaba had to grow up very quickly, and while doing so, aggression was now embraced as her best friend. Sheaba justified her aggression toward men by the multiple accounts that occurred with Walter, Bobby, and other men in her youth. Those accounts led Sheaba to becoming fearful of being overtaken and dominated by men. She refused to allow any more abuse, but bitterness germinated inside of her, which later caused unwise decisions to affect her life. Sheaba's attitude showed that she did not care what others thought about her behavior; she had to protect herself and her younger siblings from inside and outside of her home.

Rejected and Abused

Sheaba thought, *It is clearly visual that there is something wrong with that family Bobby brought into his life and those children. Why was he so blind to that? Maybe he was just as dysfunctional as they were? That family is strange, but I just cannot figure out why?* The woman Bobby was dating hid the truth of herself, but the people in her circle told her story, which related to Bobby's past. He had welcomed a family that agreed with the generational curses from his parents and their parents; those things that he devilishly carried out as a child was welcomed through laughter rather than shame. Sheba didn't know if he was abusing them because he enjoyed it, or because he learned it in his childhood. Either way, it was all bad. Sheaba cringed at the thought. It was clear that Bobby shared a relationship with a family that connected to his eroticism.

Bobby showed himself to be weak, a side of him that Sheaba had never seen. He was not loving; he was distant and an obnoxious drunk. He was angry, depressed, and stressed. Even though he still played loud music, danced, snapped his fingers loudly, and sang at the top of his lungs, there was no joy or peace as it was in the past. It was all pain covered in pretentious joy. Sheaba had become more reserved around him. She still loved him, but she despised his behavior. His presence alone brought fear to Sheaba, and spoiled their bond. To add insult to injury, he catered to a girl that was not his blood more than her. Sheaba was Jealous of Darlene in that way, but it was something she could not control. Despite the issues Sheaba had against Darlene, she tried to build a decent relationship, but Darlene always pranced around as if she was better. Often, she was the instigator of fights between Sheaba and the younger step-cousins, while she and the older step-cousins made fun of them. No one wanted to fight, but Darlene and her older cousins manipulatively forced it. They would invite Sheaba to join their conversations and then laugh at her, as if her input was stupid or made no sense. She thought she would enjoy being around them, but it was a huge letdown. *How can they be so rude, mean and thoughtless?* Sheaba wondered. That was the start of Sheaba's feelings of being inadequate, which lasted well into her adulthood. After being put down so much, she owned it.

Despite the ill treatment Sheaba received, she still loved them. All Sheaba wanted was a place of belonging, to be accepted as a sister, as part of a new family. She needed a role model, someone who would lead her in the right direction. She had already gone through a lot with the separation of her parents and to now deal with a family that was even worse than her own was heartbreaking. Hanging out with girls was no longer fun for her, hanging with the boys was more exciting. Her three eldest brothers ran away from home, and her younger brothers were not as spunky as they were. Having no choice, she made do with Darlene and her cousins or stayed in her room and listened to music or wrote what she was feeling or thinking. Their manipulative acts no longer fazed her as much as it did before. Sheaba had become more verbal in the way they were toward her. One would think the madness would end, but it didn't. It ended when she reversed the aggression toward her older cousins. Whenever they tried to bully her, she would stand up to them showing no fear. One of them even had the audacity to say; *Oh! She is trying to act tough!* Sheaba stood her ground and waited for any one of them to jump bad. No one made a move. Suddenly, the bullying stopped, and they began to treat Sheaba with kindness and respect, which resulted in her building a close relationship with one of the older cousins.

Sheaba had gotten over that hurdle only to encounter another. Sheaba made an attempt to understand what caused her dad to be so mean and evil, but it was not easy. He would never talk about the dark side of his childhood. His conversations regarding his past always stemmed around his college friends and experiences. After reaching out to Bobby's siblings and picking their brains, Sheaba gained minute understanding, but not enough to explain why he allowed himself to be mistreated by Grace and her family. However, it did explain why he was not capable of raising a family or having a healthy marriage. Sheaba often wondered why he took so much grief from Grace and her family. It was later said that he was being a gigolo. They always talked negatively about him and made him a laughing stock, a flunky, and a pushover, until he would get overboard angry and start tearing up things; then they would leave the house for a few days.

Grace, her family, and friends mocked Bobby the most when he was intoxicated. He adapted to the sneering and taunting, but never was able to deal with Grace leaving the house. When she would leave, it was for days and sometimes weeks. Although Sheaba disliked Bobby, she still respected him as her father, and she hated watching him be mistreated. *Maybe he does not care how they treat him*, she thought. He treated his children the way this new family treated him, rather than showing love so he could receive it in return. Nevertheless, he sacrificed his children's happiness for his own.

Sheaba was embarrassed that Bobby allowed the neighborhood and everyone in his new family to see that he cared nothing for his children. Even though the people in the neighborhood knew he was mistreating his children; they were too afraid to help. Bobby had clout in the neighborhood, he did behind the scene stuff for many of the unlawful organizations and they took care of him. However, any lies he sold to them were believed. He made it appear as if he were providing tough love to his children, but he showed more patience with the neighborhood kids than his own. He wanted to be well liked, and always got what he was after. A few families in the neighborhood would ask secretly about little things they observed, but Sheaba kept her mouth shut. They observed him, Grace and her children wearing the latest fashion, while Sheaba and her siblings wore second-hand clothing or walked around with clothes and shoes that did not fit, and they were filled with holes. Bobby did not have a job; he received public aid for Sheaba and her siblings, but never used it wisely. Sheaba understood the house was filled with a lot of people and everyone had to eat along with other needs that had to be met, but never understood why he did not meet his children's needs? Sheaba assumed he received a hefty public aid check and food stamps and only had rent and utilities to pay, which was cheap. There were no cars or car notes, or anything else that prevented him from clothing his children properly.

Sheaba learned to do without until the summer when she obtained a summer job. Randall and Wesley, her younger siblings were not old enough to get their own jobs, so Sheaba did what she could for them. They could barely afford school supplies, and field trips were few and far between. It was a struggle, trying to provide for herself and her siblings and make sure her dad was happy with whatever he wanted from her summer job check. Sheaba did not want to seem selfish, as she had seen what he did to her older siblings when they got paid before they left.

Bobby's misery was so bad that he succumbed to extreme heavy drinking and refused to eat. He would stay up all night, pacing the floor, talking to himself, and often knocking things over in anger. That was his routine whenever he and Grace fought, and she refused to return home for days. Having none of the boys to impose his anger upon, he found reasons to attack Sheaba and her younger siblings. *Why is he so violently abusive toward us?* Sheaba wondered. *It's not our fault that Grace left and would not come home.* Oddly, the rage would end when Grace returned home.

One evening, Grace took off on Bobby again. Bobby left home and when he returned, he was highly intoxicated. Instead of him going to his own bedroom and getting into bed, he climbed in the bed with Sheaba. That was not the first time he did that, and she hated it. Normally, he would just fall asleep, but this time he used derogatory language that spooked Sheaba. She tried to ignore him and remained still and quiet, but he got louder and louder.

Softly, she asked, "Daddy will you please allow me to rest? I'm sorry that you're hurting."

Too drunk to realize her sincerity, he yelled, "You don't care about me! You're just like everyone else."

Sheaba thought, *If he had remained the same person he was when I was a child, I'd still be attached to him.* Sheaba said, "I wish you didn't feel that way, but right now, I'm very afraid of you."

He climbed out of her bed, angrily cursed at her, and slammed her door shut. Sheaba felt relieved but cried herself to sleep after soaking in all the hurtful words he had spoken.

The next morning, Grace returned, and Bobby was content. He sat in the living room, watching sports, while Grace stayed in the bedroom watching television. Sheaba sat next to him on the couch and inquired about his health. He answered with a nonchalant attitude, which made Sheaba feel uncomfortable, but she did not give up. She wanted to show him love since he felt that no one loved him. While reaching out to hug him, she could feel his pain, but he ignored hers. Bobby was not moved by her sincere gestures; he showed no emotion but returned the hug quickly, as if he wanted her to leave him alone. His rejection of Sheaba's affection made her feel bad. She left him in the living room and walked back to her bedroom; she was not in the mood to be outside among friends. Confused by what Bobby really wanted, she decided to let him drown in his misery and enjoy his overwhelming lonely moments.

Sheaba was still confused why he changed toward her. Shocked by the distance between them, she decided to never invade his space but forgive his outlandish behavior. She wished she could heal him, but he was too stubborn to recognize he needed help.

Bobby never got better; he continued to get drunk and be obnoxious. Sheaba wasn't sure why she became his target, but she developed a fear of him. It was time to get away from the house to clear her mind. With his approval she would spend nights at her step-cousin house or her best friend that lived in the same complex. It was hard to consider leaving her younger siblings at home with Bobby; she knew that he would hurt them while she was away. Fortunately, when she returned, the boys were fine, and Sheaba was content. Her fear of Bobby turned into revulsion and disgust, which was turning into hatred. Whenever she looked at Bobby, he looked like a stranger, and unpleasant thoughts roamed through her mind.

Although Sheaba developed a dislike for Bobby, she never anticipated that he would physically hurt her. He always used scare tactics because Sheaba was easily moved to tears. Majority of the time that was enough for him. Sheaba got whippings like everyone else but not as long or as hard as the boys. Bobby hurt her feelings countless times, but she never thought he would take advantage of her love. Unfortunately, in his drunkenness he played on her emotions. He used her desire for a daddy's love to manipulate her and betray her trust.

That night, Bobby came home late in the night, entered her bedroom, and laid in the bed next to her; his comments to her were vulgar and repulsive. Sheaba knew if she refused to get help immediately, she would be in a terrible situation. The things he said made her feel like she was a piece of meat.

She screamed—but only in her thoughts—*I am your daughter! What are you doing?* Her voice trembled with fear as she said, "Daddy I love you. Please stop!"

That night his hands were roaming as he violated her space and her body. Sheaba got up and ran to the bathroom. He did not follow her right away, but he eventually got up and went to his bedroom. When Sheaba heard him turn on the music, she ran back into her bedroom. Terrified and in tears, Sheaba hoped he would not return. Sheaba was in awe at what her dad had done.

The next morning Grace and Darlene returned home, but Sheaba realized they were not there to stay. As a precaution, Sheaba asked Grace if she could tag along with them. They refused to take her, even after she begged. Confused, Sheaba wondered why Grace had not sensed something was wrong. *She has a daughter; why were no questions raised? Where are her motherly instincts?* Sheaba thought. In Sheaba's mind, Grace simply did not care, as she knew for certain that he was abusive to his children. Grace saw how he would beat them for no apparent reason. *Why did she pretend not to know that Bobby found reasons to take his anger and frustration out on them? How could Grace allow him to deprive his children of their needs as he took care of her children?* Sheaba thought, with tears in her eyes. Sheaba grew resentful of Grace because she never lifted a hand to protect them, at least not that Sheaba had seen.

Grace and Bobby's relationship was awkward. Sheaba was not sure why they were together. They did not appear to like each other very much, especially at family gatherings after they had cocktails. One time the altercation between the two was more than the usual argument; it got a little physical. Grace left the house again, this time longer than she normally did. Bobby also left the house and returned, as usual, overly intoxicated. He brought home more liquor with him—Wild Irish Rose and peppermint schnapps, his favorite. He stayed up most of the night playing "Why Do Fools Fall in Love?" over and over again.

Just before Sheaba dozed off, she heard her door open and knew what was about to happen. She pulled the covers over her head and prayed he would not climb in the bed, but he did. That was the worse night of her life; she had never been so violated. Sheaba wondered if he forgot that she was his child when he had gotten drunk. *Why me and not someone else on the streets?* Sheaba thought.

When Sheaba tried to scream, he covered her mouth with his large hands. She tried fighting back, but he was too strong. Suddenly he stopped and got up—she was not sure why—went into his room and closed the door. Sheaba ran into the bathroom, she was bleeding. Painfully, she cleaned herself up and returned to bed.

It was hard to sleep with him being in the bedroom next door. She feared he would return to her room. She stayed awake until darkness disappeared and the sunlight peeked through her curtains. The birds were singing, but Sheaba laid there until she heard her younger brothers get up. Protocol was to get up, wash their face and hands, brush their teeth, eat breakfast, began their chores and then go outside if they were allowed. When she heard Bobby fussing, she recognized her brothers were up performing their normal duties. He would always find a reason to fuss at them about something. She must have dozed off to sleep, because when she had awakened the house was quiet. The sun was shining even brighter, and this time she heard voices of people outside playing. Sheaba got up, performed all of her duties, and headed for the door to go outside. Just before she touched the door knob, Bobby stopped her.

"Where are you going?"

"Going outside to play with my brothers," she answered in a whining tone.

"Have you cleaned your room?"

"Yes."

He pointed to his favorite chair in the living room. "Sit down," he told her. "I want to talk." He walked into the small kitchen, that was a short distance from the living room, to complete the meal he was heating up for himself.

He began to talk loud enough for Sheaba to hear him from the kitchen, but Sheaba had no idea what he was saying because she had tuned him out. When she recognized that he raised his voice, she knew he was angry; it was then that she focused on his words. Sheaba was not sure what moved him to become so angry; pots were being slammed down and then she could hear him scurrying out of the kitchen.

Bobby quickly walked out of the kitchen, into the living room where Sheaba sat. Sheaba noticed he was walking toward her with a small silver steaming pot in his hand, he said, "I ought to pour this hot pot of rice and gravy into your lap."

Sheaba's panicky cry shortened her breath; she trembled and perspired, and he got angrier. He sat the pot down in the kitchen and charged toward her with his fists clenched. Sheaba threw her leg in the air and extended her arms to block the punch.

He caught her with a punch to the thigh. "Shut up all that boo-hooing," he said. "Now you have a reason to cry."

He hit her so hard that Sheaba's frail body bounced up from the chair. Surprisingly, she had not bruised, but the blow left her sore for quite a while. He made her sit in that chair until her bottom felt numb. She was fatigued and extremely sore from the tension of her muscles. She sat still, but her mind raced, wondering when he would let her go. Finally, he said she was excused—but she was not to go outside. Sheaba returned to her bedroom, laid down, and took a long nap. By the time Sheaba got out of bed, it was dusk; everyone was home and in separate areas of the house.

Bobby went back to his normal self, as if nothing had happened. Sheaba's life, however, changed in that moment. Her body felt different, and medical attention was needed, *but who would escort me to the doctor without asking questions?* Sheaba thought. Bobby kept the medical card in his wallet, and she dared not ask for it; he most certainly would have asked questions. Sheaba could only hope all was well with her body. Trying to use wisdom, she thought of ways to get help without causing herself more harm or calling attention to herself.

Unfortunately, she ultimately resorted to rebellion, which could have put her in more trouble than before. Bobby knew why she was rebelling, but he did not seem at the least worried. He left her feeling pathetic, unworthy, angry, bitter, and traumatized after the abuse. Her self-esteem went to an all-time low, and her emotions were all over the place; she was a wreck. Her grades dropped from A's to B's, and Bobby had something to say about that. All she could do was stand in front of him and pretend she cared. Her eyes welled with tears of bitterness as he reprimanded her on her grades. She wanted to yell back at him and tell him—in front of everyone—that it was his fault. But she walked away like a good little girl and ignored his comments.

She sat in her room feeling extremely lonely, especially now that her three older brothers had left home. It was hard to care for her two younger brothers when she had her own hard situation to deal with. Knowing that it was a possibility that Bobby would abuse the little ones, she was confused at what to do; but, she selfishly conjured up a plot to run away.

Sheaba's mind raced as she remembered the consistent fondling and incest, which sparked such anger in her. Then tears flowed heavily. She often felt as if anyone who looked at her saw her as a target. It was extremely uncomfortable, but she did not know how to stop it. Sheaba stayed in her bedroom often, buried in her shame. The only time she would smile was at school. Hiding her pain, she would go about her school day as if nothing happened. After school, she took her time getting home. The closer she got to the house, the more fear would rumble in her stomach, literally making her feel sick; it was so strong she almost passed out. *There must be someone who will help*, she thought. Sheaba knew she had to choose the right person, and she had to do it quickly.

Nothing ever changed around the house. Bobby and Grace repeated the same cycle, and things got worse for Sheaba. Grace continued to refuse to help her, and Bobby continued to verbally disrespect her when he got drunk. One evening during a bad thunderstorm, Bobby shut off all the lights, and everything that was run by electricity; as he believed he would be struck by lightning, he was superstitious that way. Grace and Darlene had gone to a party to which Bobby was not invited. He did not get drunk or angry, as he knew they would return after the party. Robert and Wesley were in their shared bedroom, and Sheaba was in her bedroom. The house was extremely quiet, suddenly, Sheaba heard footsteps and was hoping someone was going to the bathroom, which was next to her room. Her bedroom door swung open and hit the wall. Sheaba began to scream, she knew what was about to happen.

Bobby dragged her out of her bedroom and into his bedroom, shut the door, and locked it. She kicked and screamed and tried hard to make it impossible for him to succeed. He put a pillow over her face and began smothering her; he knew she was claustrophobic. Sheaba almost passed out, but Bobby did not get up. Before he finished, Randall and Wesley clearly having heard Sheaba's screaming, began beating on the door and yelling, "Daddy please let my sister go!"

"Go back to your room!" Bobby yelled, "before I come out and beat you!"

When he finished with Sheaba, he removed the pillow from her face, fixed his clothes, and left the room. Feeble, angry, ashamed, and helpless, Sheaba tried to get out of the bed and clothe herself, but she was afraid to get up and leave the room. She sat on the side of the bed and thought of murdering her father. The longer she sat, the angrier she had become. Without realizing it, she yelled out, "I ought to kill you!" After realizing what she said, she grabbed the Bible from the top of the headboard, held it against her body, closed her eyes, and began to cite the Ten Commandments—at least as much as she could remember. She had no clue how to pray, but she did the best she could while tears streamed down her face.

Bobby burst into the bedroom, terrifying her even more. He was waving a butcher knife and yelling, "Here! Take the knife and kill me if that's what you want to do!"

"No!" Sheaba screamed at him. "The Bible says 'thou shalt not kill'!" Sheaba did not know where the Ten Commandments were in the Bible, but she remembered when her grandmother took her to Sunday school, that is where she learned the scripture. Bobby walked away, and Sheaba made a mad dash to her bedroom. The pain she felt in her bottom was worse than the first time. It felt as if someone had taken a knife and scraped her insides. A few weeks later, Sheaba started her cycle for the first time. No one was there to show her what to do, so she sat in the bathroom and cried. Finally, she got up enough nerve to tell Grace about it, and she gave Sheaba the necessary things to take care of it. Of course, Grace told Bobby, and he acted as if it was an exciting time in Sheaba's growth into womanhood.

Sheaba cringed at the sound of his voice while making his statement about her issue. Sheaba wasted no time planning her getaway; it was impossible for her body to take any more abuse.

The man she once loved so dearly, she now deeply hated. Yet again, her heart had been broken by this man; he had become her worst nightmare and had changed her life forever. It was painful recognizing that he had protected her from the outside world because he wanted her for himself.

Sheaba decided on a plan and a back-up plan. Sheaba's math teacher was very fond of her and had invited her to spend some time with her over the weekend. Bobby gave Sheaba permission to go, but the teacher kept rescheduling the date, so Sheaba had to use her back-up plan, which was to visit her great-auntie, whom she trusted, but that backfired as well. Sheaba waited patiently and planned another day to visit her great auntie. Instead of going home after track practice, Sheaba went to her great-aunt's house, but when she arrived, Bobby, Grace, and Darlene were there. Sheaba nearly fainted when she saw them, and her stomach turned upside down. Great-Aunt Chelsea noticed how stressed she looked and invited her to her room to lie in her bed to rest. Bobby must have deduced her plan because he left the house. Sheaba then told Great-Aunt Chelsea all that had been going on; she didn't tell about the others who had abused her, only that Bobby had.

Grace and Darlene listened while she explained the situation in detail. When Sheaba was finished, Grace said that Bobby had gone to the corner store, and she would talk with him about the matter upon his return. Sheaba cried herself to sleep and must have slept for hours, as it was pitch-black outside when she woke up. Great-Auntie Chelsea was still sitting in the same spot in the bedroom as she was before Sheaba went to sleep. When she saw Sheaba was awake, she placed her hand on Sheaba's forehead to make sure she was not feverish.

"Did … *he* return?" Sheaba asked. "Has anything been resolved?"

"No," Chelsea said. "Lie back and relax."

"I cannot go back to that house," Sheaba said. "I'm afraid of what will happen to me for telling."

Great Auntie-Chelsea tried comforting her with words of affirmation, "baby everything is going to be fine. If things get too bad, you can always come back here until its resolved." But that was not going to save Sheaba from the monster in her life.

Grace returned but without Bobby.

"Did my father admit what he did?" Sheaba asked.

What came out of Grace's mouth broke Sheaba's heart even more and raised such a fear that her first instinct was to run from the house in whatever direction and never look back. Grace said, "You will return home and stop accusing people because you want to be grown."

Speechless, Sheaba sat on the side of Great-Aunt Chelsea's bed, feeling miserable and fearful. *There must be another way,* she thought. *If I must go back to that house, somebody is going to die.*

It was by the grace of God that Sheaba did not have to spend another night at that house—her two oldest brothers, Howard and Duane, showed up. Wherever Bobby had gone, Grace had gone to meet him, so they had no idea that Howard and Duane were there. Sheaba ran to Howard in tears and hugged him tightly. Darlene also ran to greet them, as if she were oblivious to what was going on. Karen, Darlene's first cousin, was very close to Sheaba, it was great Aunt Chelsea's only child; she was always with Sheaba after finding out what happened to her.

"What's wrong, Sheaba?" Howard asked. sounding frantic. "You're trembling."

Sheaba started to explaining the story again, but before she could finish, Duane furiously grabbed her hand and led her to the car. Howard and Duane talked for a few seconds, waved goodbye to Darlene and Karen, and took Sheaba home to get as many of her things as his car would hold. Then they escaped to Alabama.

When they arrived, Sheaba was overwhelmingly fatigued, so Howard set her up on his couch to rest. He did not let anyone know she was there, as he did not want her to be bombarded with questions. The atmosphere in Howard's house allowed her to feel at peace. Finally, she had escaped the madness, but she was not happy that she had left her baby brothers to deal with the monster alone. Still,

Sheaba did not look back. She only hoped that Bobby would finally learn his lesson and have mercy on his last two children.

As time went by, Sheaba received bad news that her baby brothers had chosen the wrong path and faced all kinds of vicious situations. They were being hunted by gun slayers; ones that killed for a living. It was so bad they were run out of their home and the neighborhood for fear of being murdered. *Oh my! What did Bobby allow them to get in to? How did he allow them to get in that mess?* Sheaba thought. Thank God they were able to escape and make it out alive. The good news was that a few years after Sheaba's departure, Wesley and Randall moved to Alabama to join her and the older brothers. Sheaba was content in knowing they were safe, but for her, the issues were fresh in her mind and still burned deep inside.

For years, Sheaba's past haunted her, and she began having nightmares. In those dreams, she was distraught as she had observed her father's head stuck in the roof of a vehicle after a tragic car accident. That same dream continued into adulthood, and she never understood why she was haunted by that dream. By the time she was in her late thirties, the nightmare stopped recurring. She believed Christ released her from those dreams and had given her peace.

CHAPTER 2

A Tough Life

A Life of Promiscuity

Before Sheaba escaped to Alabama, she surrendered to her vulnerability, promiscuity, and unimaginable lustfulness. There was no need to fight, as it was not painful; it actually felt good, but she knew it was wrong and very shameful, which led her into depression. What was she to do when the urges tempted her? To go outside of that home to satisfy the urge was to get beaten for what supposed family was doing to her on the inside. She allowed them to have their way with her, and she wanted it. Bobby was an exception—that was the most disgusting thing she had ever experienced. She never uttered a word about the others who touched her, so they would more than likely deny it had happened.

Sheaba battled with making good choices daily. The road she was treading was a dangerous one. She allowed other people within the family to grope her for money. As she grew numb to the pain of abuse, she was no longer afraid of her abusers; she made sure she got paid for allowing them to do what they wanted to do. Ashamed of her actions, but painfully angry at her situation, made her ignore the shame. *If they refuse to give me what I want, I will make life miserable for them.* Sheaba thought. They all played the treacherous game of a life, but none was better at playing than Sheaba. They taught her, she learned it, and had gotten better than them at their own game.

Sadly, her first experience with man was heartbreaking and traumatic. Saving her body for her husband was thrown out of the window. Abstinence was not something that Sheaba was interested in practicing. *I am unclean and my body is out of touch with time.* Sheaba thought. It made her crazy every time she thought about how she abused her body. Sheaba thought, *how do I live with what I allowed my father, stepsister, stepbrother, step-grandpa, and many others do to me.* Sheaba did not have the opportunity to be a little girl; what was being done to her sabotaged her youth. No one respected her youth, nor did they respect her as a person. Sheaba felt like a rag doll that they tossed from one person to another. Just as they used her body as a tool, so did Sheaba, giving her body into lust was a stress-reliever. When Sheaba tried to turn her life around and do better with respecting her body, it appeared that men had already read her life. Sheaba thought, *these guys refuse to have relational talk with me as if they have learned of my dysfunction.* Maybe she looked like her past, or her body language told her story. Although Sheaba chose to play sexual games, in her heart she just wanted someone to love and care for her.

The wounds that Sheaba bore deep in her soul were her excuse to continue her illicit behavior. There appeared to be no other way to live, and she was not educated on what it would take to end the vicious game. Sheaba thought, *When would the healing process begin? How would her outlandish thoughts be castrated? Who would stand to be her role model and teach her how to go to war with the desires of her flesh?* Sheaba understood that if she did not receive help, she would always do what felt good. It was impossible to make sense of the things that happened in her past, and her adult life was affected by it. Sheaba failed at every relationship she attempted because she was trapped by her past. She desperately needed counseling to prevent becoming an infuriated, bitter woman. In her hopelessness, she cried out to a God she didn't know, to gain wisdom on becoming a better person.

Broken Relationships

Sheaba had many experiences with a variety of different guys from eight years old until she was thirty-two. There was never a relationship, only lust. All she desired was attention from the opposite sex. Although Sheaba desired a long-term, loving relationship, she was not equipped with the knowledge of how to operate in one. She only knew how to please them one way—sexually. Television inspired her desires for a romantic relationship and then marriage because what it displayed is what she always dreamed as a little girl. Instead, she had grown up witnessing dysfunctional relationships that exemplified pain, suffering, abuse, and manipulation. That was her definition of a relationship. It took her a long time—not until she was much older—to understand that her relational "truth" was wrong.

Many of her family members felt that, after a while, she was too old to believe her idea of a healthy relationship was real. It was not her fault that her dad and many others who toyed with her innocence, were the reason she believed what she did about relationships. The neighborhood where she grew up also painted the same picture. Everybody was indulging in some form of promiscuity.

At twelve years old Sheaba had her first crush on an eighth-grader, Carter. He was short, slender with fair skin, an intelligent popular jockey, and a very well-mannered young man, which proved that he was raised well. Unfortunately, he did not share the same feelings Sheaba had for him, but he tried obliging her for a short while. Sheaba wished he would have given her an opportunity, as she was crazy about him—or so she thought. Love was not a real thing in her life then, the value of true love or what it meant to be in a healthy relationship was unclear, but she felt it would have been worth a try. Sheaba false sense of relationship expressed to her that Carter would be interested in her because of how he gave her attention. Sheaba longed for the fairy-tale love shown on television, but its fictitious attributes proved to be useless.

Carter respectfully met with Sheaba after four days of flirting and talking, and he sang Michael Jackson's "Human Nature" to her.

As he sang, Sheaba felt a warm sensation move rapidly down her spine. When he finished the song, Sheaba could tell by the look on his face that something was wrong, and her eyes welled with tears. That was when he delicately let her down—Carter held her hand, smiled and said, "Sheaba I have the utmost respect for you. You are sweet and beautiful, but now is not the time for me to be in relationship." Stunned, Sheaba smiled and said, "Thank you for being honest!" The rejection Sheaba felt made her reach back into her past. They hugged—and departed from one another.

Although Sheaba felt rejected, she appreciated Carters gentlemen like gesture. *It feels good to be respected,* she thought. Instead of dwelling on the rejection, she focused on getting through grade school. School was her outlet and learning was her passion; nothing would deter her from it. Two years later, she finished middle school with honors and graduated to high school without thinking of being with a boy.

In her freshman year of high school, Sheaba dated a Junior, Jason, who was a basketball player. He stood six foot five and looked like he was from Kenya, but he was indeed an American. He was very cordial, compassionate, and had a great smile. They were always together after school and after every game. As they got more involved, Sheaba took Jason to meet her family. Her brothers loved him, and her parents approved of him. Jason was impressed by the way in which her family received him, especially her dad. He wanted to come around often, but Sheaba was afraid to allow that. Her dad was crazy and always made things more than what they were. It appeared he hated any man being around her, but he pretended to like them when they came around.

Jason walked her home from school every day. Sheaba found it odd that he lived in the suburbs but was not afraid of her neighborhood. She always felt secure with him; like her dad, he had large hands that covered hers and kept her close. Although Jason was sweet and loving, Sheaba had come to realize he also was sneaky and cunning. She caught him in the stairwell of the school with a five-foot-eleven, light-skinned, bow-legged diva with beautiful long black hair. Sheaba never understood why he cheated on her, but she got through it. Surprisingly, Sheaba was not at all hurt; but, disappointed.

Prior to catching him, Sheaba had been introduced to Kelvin, a friend of her cousin Karen's. Although he was gorgeous and manly, she left it as a meet-and-greet. He was much older, but she could tell right away that he was interested. After Jason cheated on her, she decided to see what Kelvin was all about. Jason tried to make things right—they had been together for about eighteen months—but Sheaba was no longer interested. He eventually transferred to a different school.

Later, Kelvin and Sheaba fell in love and began seeing each other often. He introduced her to his parents and child. Sheaba stayed with him overnight on the weekends when she was supposed to be at Karen's. It was wrong, but it was an opportunity to be happy and to get away from the madness at home. Kelvin was consistent in treating her like a queen. There was never a dull moment whenever they were together. She was able to relax and be at peace. When they were in public—taking a walk or going to his basketball tournaments—he kept her very close. He was never overbearing and was always gentle and soft-spoken. He never got angry with her—or if he did, he never showed it.

Karen knew how happy Sheaba and Kelvin were, so she made it possible that Sheaba spend every weekend and sometimes during the week, by her house, so the two could spend time together. Bobby trusted Karen and her mother, Aunt Chelsea, so he would always approve. Auntie Chelsea didn't play, she was a big disciplinarian, but she knew Sheaba's dilemma. Little did her dad know that Karen and Sheaba had already gotten in trouble with Aunt Chelsea; she was aware of what had been going on. She decided that if her house rules were followed, she had no issue with them hanging out. Aunt Chelsea knew what Sheaba had been going through and felt that Sheaba could let her hair down, as long as it brought no drama or disrespect to her home.

Kelvin made a difference in Sheaba's life. He was different than all the other men she experienced. The closer they had become, the more Sheaba opened herself to him, sharing her personal past and current situations. He never took advantage of her story, nor did he treat her differently. He drew closer to her and had become more protective. He was a loving, strong, compassionate family man who loved and respected Sheaba as a man should. Her biggest internal battle was that he was too old for her, and she knew Bobby would flip out. Unfortunately, her dad later found out about Kelvin, aggressively approached her about him and wanted to meet him immediately. Sheaba found Kelvin and told him what had happened; he was furious, but eager to meet Bobby, especially after Sheaba shared her trauma story. Kelvin said, "I cannot wait until I get there, he better be a man about his approach, or I will beat his old tail." Sheaba responded, "that will not be necessary. I understand he is morally wrong for the things he has done, but please do not make a big deal out of this. I do not want you to go to jail. I need you!" "I will do my best sweetheart. I just don't like the way he has been treating you," said Kelvin. "I love you Kelvin! I am sure dad will not get aggressive with you. Thank you for understanding," said Sheaba.

The day Kelvin met Sheaba's father, Bobby stood up and shook his hand aggressively and offered him a seat. Kelvin refused to sit and remained standing at the door. Bobby sent Sheaba to her room while they talked, and he would not allow her to see Kelvin out when he left. After Kelvin was gone, Bobby called Sheaba to the living room. "I do not like this man! I am forbidding you to see him again." said Bobby. Sheaba walked away and headed to her bedroom. *You are jealous that a man like Kelvin would want me and he treats me like a woman. You can't stand that we are happy. I will see him whether you like it or not.* Sheaba thought. It was clear that Bobby did not want any man to be in her life. If Bobby had not behaved the way he did toward her, she might have believed his disapproval was a typical reaction from a dad. Instead, she was disappointed by her his decision. *If he and his new family hadn't forced me to grow up,* she thought, *I wouldn't have considered being with a man at my age.*

Sheaba defiantly continued to see Kelvin. The next evening, she decided to skip cheerleading practice to spend time with him so she could find out the details of his conversation with Bobby.

But Kelvin said, "I think we should cool down for a while until Bobby gets me out of his mind."

It was a hard thing for Sheaba to swallow, but she knew it was the right thing to do. Still, not being with him caused depression and loneliness, and while they weren't seeing each other, she got involved with a football player at school. Sheaba's behavior showed that she did not like being alone; it was imperative that she had a boyfriend. Having friends were not enough. She had entered adulthood early and wanted to do adult things.

Although she went out with the football player to throw Bobby off track, she kind of liked the guy. She was not crazy about him—she still was madly in love with Kelvin—so the relationship was very short. The guy had never been intimate with a woman, and Sheaba shared that time with him. After a couple of more times of intimacy, he dumped her in the worst way. He stopped calling her or speaking to her at school. Sheaba felt humiliated and rejected. She later realized he had left her a long time ago and had been dating another girl at school, one who was shy and quiet. He laughed and showed no remorse; after getting what he wanted. Every time they crossed in the hall, he smiled at her and would sing the song "Single Life." It was worse when he had the girl with him in the process of humiliation. She clenched her fists, pressed her lips together, and closed her eyes, praying she could keep it together.

Sheaba quickly got over him, and learned a little bit from that experience. *Oh well*, Sheaba thought, *it was not a total loss. I still have Kelvin.*

Sheaba reminded herself that Kelvin loved her to cover the guilt and shame she felt for getting involved with the football player. Kelvin was different than all the rest of the guys. He was even better than Bobby, who pretended to love her. Kelvin had a way of taking her mind off all she had gone through. His presence alone comforted her, and when he held her close, he did not have to say a word; she felt his love. He was the one, and she never wanted to leave his side. Two years strong together and there had never been any arguments. Sheaba had never challenged him or raised her voice at him; he was a listener, and he understood. He made her happy—so happy that she never thought about her past—at least not until Bobby attacked her for the last time.

Kelvin wanted to marry Sheaba. He promised that he would take care of her. "Whenever you're ready to leave home, come to me," he said.

But Sheaba knew that was a bad idea. She was still underage. He was twenty, and she was fifteen. If she had told him what had recently occurred with Bobby, it would have caused more trouble than she could handle. Sheaba didn't have the opportunity to tell Kelvin what had happened, it was best to run away without a word.

When Sheaba arrived in Alabama that summer, Howard enrolled her in school and sent her to Thelma, as he had his own family to look after. Thelma was extremely protective, but her husband, Roy, balanced that out very well. Sheaba was happy that her mother had found someone who loved her. Roy was a family man and had proven that he loved her children. He was very supportive and full of wisdom. Roy was always there to help her children whenever they were in need.

When Sheaba started school that fall, Roy made sure she had everything she needed and arrived to school safely. She attended Weber High, where she met Frank, a soccer player, who turned out to be a wolf in sheep's clothing. He pursued her on a bet that he could get the new girl. He succeeded, but it was not easy for him. She loved Kelvin and often thought of him, but she was forced to leave her old life behind and enjoy the new. Frank was far from being like Kelvin. She frantically searched her diary, trying to find Kelvin's home number, but she could not find it. After a while, she gave up searching but was disappointed. She couldn't bear staying in the relationship with Frank any longer, so she left him—but not before the girl he was cheating with approached her in the locker room to tell Sheaba what had been going on between them. Sheaba and Frank lasted a short six months.

That summer, at the end of her junior year, her brother Duane treated her to Benny Jack's nightclub, along with two other ladies. The club was in the hood, but it was the best party joint in Alabama; it was always jam-packed. Sheaba was a great house-party dancer, but she was very shy about people watching her dance. Duane grabbed her and pulled her onto the dance floor to help her loosen up. It was the happiest moment of her life—she had never been to a nightclub. Music and dancing always calmed Sheaba, so she let loose; it was her moment to release, and she did.

Duane showed her a great time, and for that she was forever grateful. While at Benny Jack's, Sheaba met Ricky. He was dark, handsome, well dressed and slim in build. He stood about five foot ten, and he smelled awfully good. "Hello Mrs. lady, may I have this dance?" said Ricky. "Sure," said Sheaba. He showed interest during their dance, but she ignored him. He was very charming, but Sheaba was not interested. As they walked off the dance floor, Ricky grabbed Sheaba's hand quickly before she got away and asked, "Can I offer you my number? It would be nice if we could get to know each other outside of this place." "Sure," said Sheaba. A few months had gone by and Sheaba had not called. After careful thought, she decided to call Ricky to see if it was worth her time. From that point, she and Ricky talked continuously.

They dated the entire summer and fell in love. Every weekend, she walked to his house from where she lived. He lived a half a mile away. Sheaba did not tell her mom the truth of with whom she was staying overnight. Thelma thought it was with one of her girlfriends. After all Sheaba had gone through, she wanted to do her own thing. Sheaba and her mother Thelma did not get off on a good start, but Sheaba respected her. However, the disrespect happened when Thelma accused her of agreeing to the acts of her dad. Sheaba could not understand why Thelma would insult her integrity in that way. It made her feel worthless. After that, Sheaba did not want to live with her anymore, as she did not want to repeat the same aggression as she did in Champaign.

Roy and Thelma would always drop Sheaba off at Ricky's house, not knowing it was to be with him. Neither of them knew she had a boyfriend. It was not long before Sheaba's lie was exposed. Roy began asking questions because the porch was always filled with people congregating. Roy was concerned about her safety, more than who she was seeing. He always called Sheaba Princey. "Princey? Are you going to be alright here? It always seems to be a lot of people hanging out at this house." said Roy. "I'm sorry Roy, rather than continue to lie, I will truthfully say that you are dropping me off to spend time with Ricky, my boyfriend," said Sheaba. Roy responded, "Go inside and get him. I'd like to meet this gentleman that is claiming my daughter!" Rick came outside to meet Roy and they shook hands. He asked Rick a few questions and then told Rick, "you had better take care of my little girl. If you do not, I know where to find you." Rick smiled and said, "Yes sir!" Roy felt better that he knew the truth, and he said; "Promise to never lie to me again. I can only protect you if you tell me the truth." "I promise!" said Sheaba. Sheaba kissed Roy on the cheek, "thanks dad!" "NO!" said Thelma angrily. "I will not be leaving her here! Get in this car Sheaba. NOW!" Roy said, "Thelma calm down, she had been coming here for over a month now and she has been fine. There is no need to stop her now, she would only sneak. At least we know where she is at all times." "Go ahead inside Sheaba, everything is ok." Sheaba went inside with Rick feeling better than she did when she had lied.

Later, Ricky was introduced to her brothers, after which she planned to move in with him. Thelma and Sheaba were not seeing eye to eye. Something had to change—she hadn't come to Alabama for a rerun of her depressed, uneventful life. Sheaba believed she was ready to take care of herself, even though she had no job and was still in High School, so she expressed to her mom that she was moving out. Thelma was shocked and disappointed in the sudden decision. "You are moving in with that boy, aren't you?" "Yes ma'am," said Sheaba. "Well, I will not stop you. I wish you would reconsider. All momma is trying to do is keep you from making the same mistakes I made with your dad." "I hope he treats you well. If you need me, you know where to find me." Sheaba was only sixteen and a half years old, and with no moral guidance, she was moving out in a world to learn to care for herself. Thelma knew she would face more hardship and wanted to hold on to her a little while longer, but it was too late. Sheaba was defiant and could see only her way, freedom.

Sheaba realized she was a runner. When things got tough, the best thing to do was to run away from the issues, rather than face them. It was hard to handle situations without fighting with her hands and her mouth. To stay with Thelma would mean she was defeated, and she hated that feeling. After her amazing outing with her brother Duane, she wanted to explore life a little more, meet people, and hang out occasionally. She loved school and loved being around people; it fulfilled her lowest moments. The town where Sheaba lived was not as small as people claimed it to be. It was difficult learning how to get around on the bus, but she was successful in figuring it out. After a year, Sheaba made attempts to find a part-time job as she wanted to be prepared to pay for her Senior fees. A local restaurant hired her, but it didn't pay enough to handle all the fees for her senior year.

Sheaba remembered, *mom said if I needed her that I knew where to find her. I will ask her for the money.* Sheaba's attempt failed. "Sheaba when you left home, you chose to take care of yourself. How come Rick is not paying for the things you need instead of asking me?" Sheaba said, "That is pretty mean mom seeing that you get financial assistance for me and I no longer live with you." Thelma said, "that money is paying the bills. Remember, you chose to leave. By the way, make sure you come and pick up the rest of your things because I am moving out of here soon." Sheaba was hurt but searched harder for a full-time or second part-time job to support herself. Ricky was not working, which made things that much harder. Ricky recognized Sheaba's pain and said he would work harder at finding a job to help. Unfortunately, neither of them was successful. Sheaba was able to pay her senior fees but was not able to participate in any of the trips or the prom, and was barely able to pay for her graduation. When Sheaba was depressed, Ricky found ways to make their relationship relaxed through romancing her and being affectionate.

Several months into her senior year, Sheaba found out she was pregnant, and things began to change between her and Ricky. Sheaba became overly emotional and unsettled with Ricky's behavior after she told him she was pregnant. Because of his change, Sheaba tried to find out more about him. She always felt he was lying to her about something, but she ignored it.

One afternoon while Ricky was napping, she went through his wallet, looking for his ID, she found it and discovered he was five years older than she was—that explained why his family always got mad at him and said he was robbing the cradle.

When he woke up, she confessed that she had gone through his wallet and looked at his driver license.

Ricky was angry about Sheaba's prying, but he also felt bad about lying to her and tried to explain. "After I fell in love with you, I didn't want to tell you my real age and risk your leaving me."

Although his answer softened her heart, she was still not happy about the lie. "Have you lied about other things?" she asked. Instead of searching for more evidence, she allowed him time to come clean on his own. Ricky said, "There is nothing more to tell. That was the only thing I kept from you. I do apologize for the lie and I will never do it again. Please do not ever snoop through my things again." Sheaba sheepishly looked at him, rolled her eyes and walked away.

Sheaba had to inform her track coach that she was pregnant and was unable to run. Running on the track team is what helped her focus on keeping her grades up. Her desire to drop out of school was at an all-time high. She and Ricky started having many disagreements and physical altercations, which forced her to face her past hurts and pain. Still, they stayed together and worked through their problems. Ricky eventually found work through a temporary service, doing odd jobs to keep money coming in—he knew eventually they would have to get their own apartment. Midway through her pregnancy, Sheaba was considered an at-risk patient and was ordered by her doctors to refrain from any strenuous work. Ricky had done his best to make Sheaba as comfortable as possible, but he was stressing about work and finding an apartment. One evening, while Sheaba and Ricky were cuddling upstairs in the family room of his cousins house, Sheaba encountered yet another one of Ricky's inability to share the truth. They were attempting to watch a movie when they heard a lot of commotion going on downstairs. They both went downstairs to check it out. Ricky was excited to see his mother and two of his sisters, but his face changed when he had seen the woman they brought with them from Champaign. That was the first time Sheaba had seen his mom and siblings. Ricky asked, "What is she doing here?" The woman stood behind Ricky's family holding a baby of about a year old. His name was DeAngelo, a cute little bundle of joy, who Sheaba had later come to adore. "What do you mean, what am I doing here?" the woman said. Rick said, "Like I said........Ricky's mom cut the argument short and introduced herself to Sheaba and then to his two sisters. She also introduced Sheaba to the woman. Ricky's mom explained that Ricky had a child born as his first.

Instead of being angry about the deceit, Sheaba felt bad for the woman; it wasn't her fault that Ricky had kept her and his son a secret. Ricky was responsible. After his secret was out, Ricky and the woman began seeing a lot of each other. She visited him, and he visited her, each in separate cities. Ricky allowed the woman to come between he and Sheaba, to the point that Sheaba felt abandoned. Eventually, Sheaba found a way to sneak a trip to Champaign, where Ricky had left Alabama and stayed there for about a week. She was angry that he would leave her alone at his family's house and embarrass her by staying with another woman. She thought, *For God's sake, I'm pregnant and haven't harped on the secret that exposed Ricky, but I get left behind. What kind of mess of a life is this?*

Ricky showed no respect—he never called to check on her or to make sure she was looked after while he was gone. He never informed her that he would be gone for an extended time; he would always just leave. Sheaba was fed up, and her behavior had become vicious, aggressive, angry, and bitter. She was tired of dealing with men and their disrespect, so she reverted to doing what she knew best—fighting. When Sheaba arrived in Champaign, she waited until she had gotten to the door of his sister's apartment to call and ask her to open the door. To her surprise, there was Ricky and the woman cuddled on the couch. Disrespectfully, they acted as if she were not there. Sheaba patiently waited for Ricky to finish his rendezvous and acknowledge her, and when he finally did, she was too tired to fight; she just listened. He went back to Alabama without her, and she did not care. She stayed another week before she returned, but when she did, her attitude toward him was different.

Sheaba called her mom to see if she was still in the same house and received permission to return home. Sheaba called brothers to help her move her items back to Thelma's place, where she stayed until the baby was born. Staying with Thelma was not as bad as before.

Sheaba was so stressed that she began to skip school. She knew she had the extra credits that were transferred from her old high school in Champaign that would be enough to allow her to graduate. Three days before graduation, Dalia was born, 6lbs, 8oz and 18 inches long. Labor was long and intense, but Sheaba was resilient. Dalia came out with one push, flying into the arms of the doctor. When the nurse brought Dalia to Sheaba, she said, "Wow Sheaba, the doctor had to take a couple of steps backward to catch her."

After suffering during the pregnancy, it was nice to experience God's creation—a beautiful, chocolate little girl. Upon Sheaba's release from the hospital, Sheaba faced a couple of issues: first, her daughter could not come home with her because she was being treated for jaundice and had a blood transfusion to keep her alive; and second, Sheaba did not have a home to go to because she had decided not to return to her mother's home. She had gotten word that Ricky was no longer welcome to return to the home of the family member where they both previously lived. Sheaba wasn't sure what happened with Ricky and his family while she was away at her mother's home, but she trusted Ricky to find a place where they could lay their heads until they got jobs to move.

Sheaba signed up for public aid to supplement them until they found work. Ricky did find another family member who allowed them to stay, and they bounced around from home to home for 3 months until they found a place to call their own. Fortunately, the place they found rent was $275 a month—very reasonable—so they were not struggling, as Sheaba received $700 per month in government money, plus $260 in food stamps. Their landlords were a wonderful young couple who had just married and recently had had a baby as well. They were happy to rent to Ricky and Sheaba and took care of all of their household needs. From that point, Ricky and Sheaba did exceptionally well, despite the relationship problems they faced. When they got settled, Sheaba signed up for college and continued her search for work. One month after they moved into their new home, she found work through a temporary service, at a factory, where she worked for several months. During that time, she got pregnant with their second child. Both Sheaba and Ricky worked hard at the same work site, but different areas, until Sheaba had to quit just before giving birth.

Ricky and Sheaba's second child, Earnest, was the cutest little soldier, 6lb 8oz 21inches long, a caramel baby who wasted no time in coming out—Sheaba's labor was relatively short, and he came out with two pushes. After a while, Ricky's weariness with the relationship began to show, and when Earnest turned three years old, Ricky left them. When Earnest was two, they had made plans to get married and had paid almost all of the wedding bills except for the rings and his groomsmen attire, and then he went "ghost" on them. Sheaba's anger caused her to put her fist through the bay window that looked out on the front porch of their home. Prior to that happening, she found out she was two months pregnant, which made her even more emotional and irrational. Instead of going directly to the hospital, she wrapped her arm with a wet bath towel, laid on the floor and went to sleep. The children were with Ricky's mother, so she did not need to worry about them, but by the time Sheaba was rushed to the hospital, she had already lost a lot of blood, and she lost the baby.

Sheaba felt defeated and downtrodden. Not knowing what to do, she reached out to Kelvin. Even after visiting him in Champaign, Sheaba recognized her feelings changed toward him. Kelvin was angry after hearing why she left Champaign. After learning that her first child was not his, he treated her with disrespect, and she never contacted him again. *I do not understand what happened with Kelvin or why he reacted that way! I thought he understood my position. I guess now I am at a total loss with men.* Sheaba thought. She felt as if all hope was lost for a happy relationship. Rejection forced her into a deeper depression where she no longer lived her life as a striving woman but as a defeated woman with low integrity and self-esteem. Sheaba's understanding of life was a blur.

One year later, Sheaba moved from the apartment she and Ricky had shared into a slightly more expensive but larger apartment. Ricky still had her heart and would come around whenever he felt like it. Sheaba was lonely, so she put up with whatever he wanted. He impregnated her again, but this time he denied the child was his before it was born.

Sheaba thought, *When will I learn my lesson about fooling around with men like him?* She didn't understand why she felt so attached to someone who did not want her in any way. Later, however, Ricky— possibly because he had run out of places to go—proposed to Sheaba again. She allowed him to move in with her and the children, but he asked if she would abort the child she was carrying, as he didn't want to walk down the aisle with a fat woman, and he had enough children. He continued to pressure her to abort the baby, and although she fought tooth and nail against the idea, she wanted to be married more than she wanted another baby.

Sheaba's young mind was distorted, and no one was around to help her fix it. She agreed to the abortion, with Ricky by her side. The abortion clinic's policy was to show a video to the mother- and father-to-be before going through the process, in hopes of changing their minds. After watching, Sheaba was sure she did *not* want to go through with it, but she did it anyway. She was traumatized for quite some time after doing it, but overtime made it through that nightmare.

Ultimately, the wedding did not happen. Sheaba thought she had no desire to be with Ricky after that horrible experience, but she went back again. However, her heart ached daily at the thought of being responsible for the death of a child and having no valid reason for having done it. Later within that same year, Ricky returned, not to renew their relationship but for shelter until he got on his feet. Sheaba thought, *I know this is a bad idea, but I refuse to allow the father of my children be homeless, regardless of how evil he had been to me.*

During the time Ricky was living with Sheaba and the children, they fought constantly, as usual, but in the process, she got pregnant again. This time she did not allow Ricky to talk her into any madness, she learned her lesson from the mental trauma she experienced. Ricky, had a date the night Sheaba told him she was pregnant. Sheaba did not care, but when she prepared to do the same, he started a big fight that caused her to call the police and get him out of her house. The children were with Sheaba's mother, so they were not exposed to the abuse. Sheaba went through her last pregnancy alone. However, the last month before Sheaba went into labor, Ricky showed up. That week she went into labor while he was visiting. Ricky went with her to the hospital but did not sign the birth certificate as the father.

Lamont came into the world after two pushes. He was beautifully bright, unlike the first two who were gorgeously dark, weighing 6lbs 120z 19 inches long. His eyes were squinty and tight, and had a head full of hair. He was not crying when he was born, so the doctor slapped his bottom. Two months after Lamont was born, Sheaba moved again. It was time to stop having kids by Ricky and get her life in order. Ricky was always allowed to visit the children, but with third party supervision, away from her home. Sheaba took Ricky to court to establish paternity of Lamont; she was tired of him denying her son. Lamont was ten years old when the paternity test was administered and proven that he was the father. By then, Ricky was married to a woman who hated Sheaba and who took every opportunity to make Sheaba feel like a terrible person. It took Ricky a while to accept that Lamont was his child and to include him, but Sheaba made sure Lamont was not forgotten.

At age twenty-two, Sheaba was a full-time single mom of three, struggling to make ends meet. Determined to do better with her life decisions, she made strong efforts to give as much attention to her children in their infancy as she could. Her thoughts would roam at times into places of darkness, that made her feel mentally unstable. Instead of allowing those thoughts to control her, she reminded herself of the three beautiful children that God had given her. Years prior to having children, she asked the Lord for them, and asked if they can love her the way she love people. He fulfilled that promise. It was not always easy raising them alone, but she fought to make sure she did not let them down or God. Sheaba needed counseling, someone who was not professional but was filled with wisdom. Paying for a therapist was not an option—it was too expensive.

Only God could change her life. God was still a mystery to her, but she understood he was a Savior. She was frustrated that she didn't know the steps for seeking him; she didn't know how to pray and wondered if he would hear her, as she was so filthy. Her grandmother had introduced her to God when she was younger, but she never understood the purpose. Likewise, her Aunt Chelsea had taken her to a sanctified church when she was a pre-teen, where everyone carried themselves kind of weird. They were speaking a weird language and falling on the floor. She never understood what that was all about, and she never tried it. What she did do was dance, which she thought was considered the Holy Ghost at that time. She danced only so she could fall on the floor and go to sleep, and someone would cover her with a thin cloth blanket. This type of worship continued until a prophet gave her a Bible for her birthday, and she began to read it for herself.

Reading the bible made no sense, but it sparked her curiosity because she was prompted by a preacher to join Bible trivia on Wednesday nights. After joining, she practiced daily reading, which lead her to winning the Bible-trivia games. Great-Aunt Chelsea was proud of her for taking those bible study classes she taught seriously; she said it paid off. Her and her cousin Karen did not only read, but they were expected to be able to explain the scriptures they read and apply it to real world events. After Great-Aunt Chelsea passed away, Sheaba put the Bible down and continued her lost life.

Great Aunt Chelsea taught bible life application, but Sheaba was still a beginner when she died and had forgotten a lot of what she was taught. When she stopped reading the Bible, she lacked the understanding of the scriptures. Having no other guidance in assisting her with navigating her life, ignorantly, she got involved in more detrimental relationships. That is, being with men who were toxic but camouflaged as healthy. Sheaba esteemed her men and anyone who accepted her as a friend more highly than herself. It was evident she did not love herself, know herself, her worth, or her purpose. *What did that even mean? How does a person love themselves? What does that look like? I know enough to get by, what more do I need to know about myself? I take care of my kids, and I protect them. How do I find out what more I need to do?* Sheaba thought. *Growing up, everybody acted as if they hated each other, there was no love,* Sheaba thought. There was so much trauma in the house Sheaba live in with Bobby in her childhood years, that the only love she knew was her pride and education. Well, she did love her siblings, but that was not considered loving herself.

Because Sheaba did not know how to love herself, her heart was numb to the truth of real love. Being deceitful, malicious, and bitter was the norm, it took the place of love. Whatever her heart told her to do, she did it, and she allowed herself to be controlled by it. Whatever played out in her mind, she performed it and did it well, good, or bad. Very few things ever backfired on her, as everything was carefully thought out. At times Sheaba was emotionless toward everything except for her children and her immediate family. Love to Sheaba was lust, and men dominated her in that way by unleashing charming words and gifts. Her heart was always broken from the deception, yet she always bounced back and repeated the same cycle. Her academic IQ was great, but her social ability to comprehend the minds of men was far below average.

Sheaba resulted to excessive partying denying her duties as a full-time mother. Drinking, smoking cigarettes and marijuana became habitual. During that time she met many men. Some thought she was dumb. Dumb enough to dance for money, while others thought she was an easy sexual fix. Sheaba was not that naïve, but she loved men. Sheaba had a little class – inadvertently, she did not date any type of man. She desired men of class but did not present enough class to grasp that type of man. Her bitter and broken life always came out in conversation and ran them away. Low self-esteem fit her body better than her curves in a bodysuit, because only the in-between guys approached her—the ones who had their lives partially together and had a little bit of sense. Life was terrible, and she was stuck in it, but she was tenacious; every time she would fall, she would rise again.

Depression and oppression were her best friends, they embraced her faithfully. The new lifestyle she embraced, (party life) had her neglecting her mother duties more and more, but she was blinded. Men were Sheaba's opium. Whenever her best friends (depression & oppression) visited, she sought her opium (coitus), which satisfied her pain. In her address book was a list of men with whom she was comfortable being intimate; when one was not available, she'd call the next and then the next until she found one who was. When he arrived, she tore into him erotically like a savage, full of anger and bitterness. Some did not mind the aggressive passion, while others, who really cared about her, was concerned, but disassociated themselves. She always hoped an apology would suffice for her behavior, but it only made things worse. Begging them to come back gave them the power to impose disrespect, but they were to blame. Sheaba viewed them as monsters—a bad drug that caused her overdose. She was angry that they would not assuage her bitterness, so her heart grew numb toward them. Blinded by the opium, she continued to use until her pushers began to dominate through learning her past.

Men recognized the battle scars on her body that told her life story, and they questioned it. Although it was embarrassing to tell her story, she did, and she laughed as if it were a joke. Behind closed doors, however, she would mourn. The open door to her secret that began her opium habit, hid the truth of her innocence, and made her feel like a harlot. No one understood her pain, fear, or anger because Sheaba never expressed the constant rape. Although she should have been called a harlot, God hid her until she allowed him to gain control of her life. When God spoke to her, she could not hear because she allowed the opium(coitus) to stand in the way.

Sheaba eventually grew weary of the club scene and started having "weekend specials" at Ricky's first cousin Iyana's home. Iyanna was Sheaba's club partner and had developed a bonded relationship. Home rendezvous allowed her to be closer to her children, rather than leaving them with a babysitter all the time. During one of those gatherings, Sheaba met Gerald, whose family lived below Iyana. It just so happened Gerald was having a family gathering that day. Iyana was friends with them, so she took Sheaba down to meet the family. Gerald and Sheaba locked eyes. He had a chocolate complexion, stood six foot four, bow-legged, and well dressed. "*Definitely eye candy,*" she thought. *And he smelled so good.* Gerald was more appealing than the men who were standing by, waiting to be chosen. Iyana said he was multitalented, a mentor to his nieces and nephews, and independent. Sheaba immediately caught his attention and reeled him in.

After the company left, Gerald asked, "would you mind staying here with me? I would like to get to know you." Sheaba, slightly intoxicated said, "Of course!" Surprisingly, he did not force himself on her and neither did she. They did cuddle on the living room floor the remainder of the evening, sharing stories. Sheaba was moved by the fact that Gerald was more interested in her than the plans he made with his friends. He ignored the phone calls and his constant vibrating pager. He gave Sheaba his undivided attention. They did not waste time engaging in a romantic relationship, which went very well the first year. In the middle of year two, Gerald began to change. He wanted to share himself but wanted Sheaba to be with him alone. He wasn't giving her the same attention he had, and he only had her over to his place at his expense.

One evening Sheaba called Gerald to let him know she would be staying at his place after the house gathering at Iyana's. Iyana dropped her off but did not leave until she was able to get into the building. Iyana got out of the car when she had seen Sheaba standing at the door for a while. Gerald was ignoring the bell, so she rang his neighbor's door who buzzed her and Iyana inside. Sheaba knocked on Gerald's apartment door and opened it with the burglar chain on and peeked out. Sheaba's anger went into overdrive, and she kicked the door in. Gerald ran to the bedroom in his boxers. Iyana pushed past him and ran to Gerald's bedroom first and turned on the light. There, she found another woman, undressed and lying in his bed.

"Stay there if you don't want to be attacked by Sheaba," Iyana advised the woman.

Surprisingly, Sheaba was calm after seeing the woman in Gerald's bed and turned to leave. But Gerald grabbed her by the neck to provoke her to fight, Sheaba refused to engage. Iyana grabbed Sheaba, and they both ran out the door.

Sheaba forgave him but refused to leave him alone—and things got worse. She nearly incapacitated him for putting his hands on her in front of her children. The police were called, and Sheaba was afraid she was going to jail. Fortunately, Gerald did not press charges; he asked the police to issue a warning. She was barred from his property and was not to go near him.

Enough was enough; Sheaba decided to take her children and move back to Champaign. It was a great decision, as it was time to face her past and move on to a positive life.

When Sheaba and her children arrived in Champaign, Darlene and her husband, Benny, picked them up from the train station. Sheaba believed that, over time, her childhood hurts were rehabilitated, and she could handle the relationship with Darlene. The first month there was great, and Sheaba appreciated every moment. The only problem she faced at that time was enrolling her children in school. Champaign made it hard because it was the middle of the school year. Sadly, Sheaba had to send her children back to Alabama with Thelma to enroll them in school. Sheaba had started college and was unable to return with her children at that time.

Sheaba was doing well in school and was excited to find something better to do with her life. Being in school and exercising was an excellent outlet; it inspired positive thoughts. Gerald called often but Sheaba ignored him. Gerald feeling angry and rejected drove to Champaign, but Benny, her brother-in-law, protected her from the madness. After that, Sheaba was content that she heard nothing from Gerald. Sheaba's dedication to class showed from the grades had received. Exercising was paying off; her body dedicated to focusing on school, and exercising was paying off. She was pleased with her body and how healthy she felt.

Benny often got up in the morning when Sheaba was up for school, so he would drop her off on his way to work. They shared stories of despair and comforted one another; he was a great person to talk to. The routine continued every morning and they had become the best of friends. While Sheaba was appreciating their friendship in a respectful manner, he had become emotionally attached. Once, in the wee hours of the morning, Sheaba felt her desires heighten and thought it was a dream, as she had not experienced that feeling in a while. When she opened her eyes, Benny was there, he had already made her reach her peak so she didn't resist. Sheaba had never been awaken that way; and it played in her mind often. Benny did not leave her alone; Sheaba felt bad at first because she had given up opium for a while. Unfortunately, she relapsed and the desire to have it returned. Benny suggested using another location, having no shame for his actions. Sheaba, at first, felt bad, but then she reflected on the trauma she inflicted upon her in her childhood. Sheaba felt Darlene deserved the payback for ruining her life, and this was her way of retaliating. Her blaming Darlene, however, was her excuse, but Sheaba knew it would eventually backfire. Still, she did not care at the time. When they did not get caught, Sheaba stopped their encounters, as she felt it was enough. Benny understood and never bothered her again, but they remained respectfully close.

After eight months, Sheaba returned to Alabama; she missed her children. Moving back with her mom was not easy, because she loved her own space. Thelma was awesome during that time; she was nothing like she was growing up. When Sheaba found a place, Benny came down to help her move her items.

Darlene did not find out about the affair between her husband and Sheaba until three years later. Darlene called Sheaba to discuss the matter, but Sheaba cut it short by apologizing and explaining her malicious reason behind it. They did not speak to each other for many years, but Sheaba still didn't allow it to affect her; she was still holding a grudge. What was done could not be undone, so she moved on.

Two years after returning to Alabama, Sheaba met Greg, who was approximately nine years older, divorced, tall, fair-skinned, nicely built, and mellow. He was not the typical guy that she would normally go for. He was the serious type; he had no children; he lived alone and worked multiple jobs. Sheaba feared she would fall for him quickly, so she worked hard at staying out of his path. She was not looking to get another quick fix.

Sheaba worked out a lot, so she ran into him at the gym often. They were never officially introduced, nor did they ever have a conversation; he would just wave and smile. Then Greg met her outside the gym one afternoon and asked if he could drop her off at home; she declined. He was persistent for a while, but Sheaba continued to decline, so he stopped asking.

On another occasion, Sheaba and Greg ran into each other at a local grocery store near the gym. As she entered the store, she had seen Greg standing in one of the aisles. Sheaba thought she looked a mess, so she tried to avoid him, but they bumped into each other in another aisle. She waved quickly and made a mad dash to the register to get out of the store before he caught up with her again. She successfully made it out of the store and quickly walked to the bus stop. Unfortunately, when Greg left the store, she was still standing at the bus stop. Greg pulled alongside her and asked if he could drop her off at home. She accepted this time, as it was a bitter cold day, and she wanted to get home before her children got out of school. They rode in silence at first, but then Greg asked, "How have you been?"

"Isn't it obvious?" she snapped.

He shook his head, not understanding what she meant, so she lowered the hood of her jacket and pointed at her face. Her eyes were swollen from crying on her way to the store—she had been looking back over her life and saw that nothing had really changed. It was a bad time to talk to him; she was an emotional wreck, but he was so persistent that she got tired of running. She hoped he would decide to run away and leave her alone afterward, but it only drew him closer. Apologetic to her circumstance, he opt to listen to her vent.

For a moment she sat quietly while the tears streamed down her face. When she finally opened her mouth to talk, aggression and anger took over like a bad habit. Greg saw her overwhelming frustration and volunteered to let her punch him to get rid of some of the aggression. Instead, she started punching his dashboard with her clenched fist. After she was done, they both laughed hysterically. By that time, he was pulling up in front of her house. As he parked, Sheaba was embarrassed because the front of the duplex and the porch was filled with kids. The entryway door was wide open, and the block looked like a tornado had blown garbage everywhere. They sat in the car for a while, talking, before he gave her his number and asked her to call him. She was shocked! How could he want to talk to a mad woman after hearing all her painful woes and complaints, beating his car, and seeing that where she lived was fairly ghetto.

Several months went by, but Sheaba did not connect with Greg. Sheaba had a bad habit of setting down numbers written on paper and losing it. However, later she would find it. Fortunately, she did find Greg's number in the Livingroom cabinet while dusting. She called to see if the number still belonged to him, and he answered. When she nervously introduced herself, he chuckled and said, "Hello, stranger." They stayed in contact via phone for about two months before he asked her out. She knew he was old-fashioned because everyone else took her to their homes first. Greg knew how to court a woman, and Sheaba felt like she had found a winner.

Sheaba was used to men introducing to her their opium; somehow, they sniffed her out and reeled her in. She was happy that Greg was not interested in selling his opium, and she agreed to the date. Later, he took her to his home, where he led her to his living room and turned on some Anita Baker, and then made dinner. After eating and having good conversation, he drove her home. Not once did he make any advances toward her to entice her habit.

They enjoyed a few more dates before Greg decided he wanted to make her his lady. He invited her to a Super Bowl party given by his place of employment. There, as they danced, he asked her to be his lady. She looked him in the eyes to see if he was being genuine or lustful. He never tried to come on to her, but she wanted to be sure he was not manipulating her. This was a new approach, one that Sheaba had never seen before, and that kind of treatment was sure to trigger her opiate addiction. Accepting his proposal, they both smiled and embraced. Sheaba loved his clothes, his cologne, and the attention he got from other women, whom he ignored while he focused on her. That night Sheaba went home with a big smile on her face. She felt a sense of satisfaction and relief in knowing that a man like him was interested in her basket case of a life. It baffled her that he would choose her, but she thought, *Why question it?*

It was kind of awkward moment, as she had not been with anyone that much older since Kelvin, nor had she been with anyone for a long time, who exemplified gentlemen like gestures as he did. Sheaba figured this was a good opportunity to prove that she could defeat her past. Sheaba thought, *Maybe, Kelvin would understand her past and help her work through it.* Regrettably, while dating Greg, Sheaba experienced hardship and ended up in a homeless shelter. In the meantime, Greg asked, "Sheaba, I'd like to take you out again if that is ok with you?" Sheaba said, "I apologize Greg, I will have to decline this time." She could hear his tone change when she declined. "Why?" said Greg. "Something has come up that I do not feel comfortable exposing to you at this time." said Sheaba. He did not give up. "What could be so wrong that your man could not handle for you? Who am I as your man, if you cannot trust me to do what I need to do on your behalf to help you? Why am I your man Sheaba? Sheaba had become emotional at Greg's persistent and forthright questions. "Ok! Ok!" said Sheaba. "My children and I are in a shelter on the south side of town because I was unable to make payment of my rent. I lost my job when I got sick. The doctors told me I was unable to return to work for at least three weeks. My boss tried to hold my job for me, but she needed help immediately." Sheaba was embarrassed, but, hoped she would not be judged or pitied by Greg.

The next day Greg came to visit Sheaba and her children at the shelter with a plan. He took them out for a nice dinner and a movie. Feeling nervous about the time they'd spent—she didn't want to lose her bed at the shelter—she explained the rules of the facility to Greg.

"Greg, I thank you so much for this kind gesture, and I would love for things to be different, but they are not. The shelters policy is that we return by 8:00 p.m. or we lose our bed. Will you please take us back?"

"Sheaba, I won't allow my lady to live in a place like that, and I would like you and the children to stay with me until you get on your feet."

She had a choice to make: stay in the shelter and lose her man, or keep her man and suffer the consequences of moving in with him. Sheaba was nervous but ignored it. She could have said no and returned to the shelter, but she did not want to. Still, it was not a good idea to move in with him.

Sheaba smiled at Greg and said excitedly, "Greg are you serious? I….I don't know if that is such a good idea, and I know I have a choice, but…… Greg cut her off and said, "Baby, let me help."

Sheaba and Greg went strong for about a year, but then, somehow, the relationship took a turn for the worse. Sheaba must have gotten the communication mixed up. She was sure Greg told her to make herself comfortable. But Greg was not happy with the changes made to his place. One day, while Greg was at work, Sheaba thought she would re-decorate his place with some of her décor. Doing so, made it feel more like home. *After all, it was a bachelor pad with no flavor to it,* she thought. Sheaba sensed discomfort in his actions and choice of words.

His response was very hurtful: "I feel as if you are refusing to prepare to move out and get your own place. I never said once that you were to be here indefinitely, so why are you unpacking as if I did?"

At that moment, Sheaba felt rather stupid for choosing to move in with him and for trying to make the house comfortable. Innocently, without a thought of remaining there, Sheaba wanted him to experience a woman's touch to his place. Immediately the next day, Sheaba removed all of her decorations and put everything back the way Greg had it prior to her arrival. Later, when Greg returned home from work, he noticed Sheaba removed her things and asked, "Hey Sheaba, why did you remove everything, you could have left it.? Sheaba thought, *how odd it is for him to be concerned after his outlandish behavior about it before.* Clueless and confused at what he wanted, she sat there like a child, trying to figure out how to respond. Sheaba said, "I thought that is what you wanted." Greg did not ask again, and Sheaba never mentioned it or redecorated again.

Sheaba's confidence in knowing the direction she should take to remove herself and the children out of their situation was not clear. Her unclear understanding of who she was and what Greg wanted, unleashed stress. Sheaba thought, *was Greg trying show her a better life, and at the same time trying to control it, or am I just a dreamer, hoping for something that does not exist.* Sheaba looked at the fact that she has three children, with no job, single, no goals, and was at times irresponsible. Sheaba thought, *wow, I am a target to be controlled. But there is not a man that can strong arm me. I am as strong as they are and will retaliate if I need to.* Her view of life was horrible; God could not have had her in his plan for happiness. Sadness was all she had ever known and embraced from a child to adulthood. It was hard to determine if it was her own self-inflictions or if she was destined for pain. Sheaba hated who she had become and despised her life. To stay that way would be detrimental to her children's growth. *There had to be a way to escape the madness,* she thought, *but how?* Having no desire to bounce her children around anymore, she allowed Greg's control mechanisms until she found another home.

Greg was not argumentative, but he was very sarcastic and judgmental. He always found ways to push Sheaba's buttons, and she would react just as he knew she would. His behavior reminded her of dad, who made coming home from school horrifying. There was always that moment when she or her brothers walk through the door, they would get beat upon walking in. Sheaba never knew what mood Greg would be in when he got home from work, so she would speak to him and keep moving. Although he took care of her and the children, she no longer considered him to be the nice gentleman that she remembered.

Sheaba thought, *Greg is not a bad person; he sacrificed a lot for her and the children. He opened the doors to his home even though I had no job. When I did find one, he gave me his car to use to keep me and the kids out of the cold. He even opted to buy me a car. He changed his mind when I changed, I guess.* Greg purchased another vehicle for himself and allowed her to continue driving the old one— and he took responsibility for the maintenance of both vehicles.

Sheaba's having a job made things a bit simpler for herself and the relationship. Greg appeared to have fallen back in love with her, he even begun talking marriage and having kids. Sheaba was ok with the marriage, but having kids was not what she was able to offer him. Although she desired to give him children, prior to meeting him she had a tubal ligation. Greg had been married prior to their relationship but had no children. *I am sure Greg will leave me once he realizes I am unable to bear his children,* Sheaba thought. Sheaba wanted to be like her mother and have children with only one man. Sheaba was fertile and she knew if she had not gotten the procedure done, she would have had multiple baby daddy's; her addiction would not have allowed her to tell her pushers "no!"

Marriage was great, but Sheaba was not equipped for it. Sheaba thought, *marriage requires a different kind of love and with my temper and aggression, I am sure to ruin it.* Sheaba had not learned her place as a woman, being typically masculine was more familiar. *Marriage meant that I would have to be confident, strong-minded, without debt, a virgin and have a career, none of which I have,* Sheaba thought. Sheaba's self-esteem was low, and her self-confidence was nonexistent. She had loads of debt and three small children to raise. *Who would do what Greg is doing for me, knowing all of that? Why would he want to marry me and have kids?* Sheaba thought. Greg had worked two jobs for a long time. He had exceptional credit; he was responsible, confident, and had his life in order. Allowing Greg to marry her past would be cruel and unfair. Sheaba was sure that she could not love him the way he needed to be loved.

In addition, Greg despised her mother and was not fond of her brothers, so life not only would have been miserable but unfair to him—and to Sheaba as well. Sheaba loved her mother and brothers; they were her best friends. They had countless family gatherings, and she knew Greg would not be interested in joining her. Having Greg by her side at those family gatherings was important to Sheaba. Greg appeared to be socially awkward, so he would not have been a good fit for marrying. Sheaba was right, Greg did not take the news well that she could not have children and that was important to him. Again, he began to act as he was before, different in a way that ruined their relational bond.

Sheaba's emotional madness in relationships had to be dismissed, if she was considering leading a better life for her children. After having children, she thought that her past hurts would go away, but realized she was wrapped in a life of a generational curse. The only man she needed in her life was not of the flesh but of the spirit. Sheaba thought, *I do not know why I believe that, but it feels right. I have never seen anybody changed by living for God. Why do I believe he will do it for me?*

The choice to move out of Greg's house, was the best choice she had made. It was the first step toward a changed life. *Being with Greg is a hindrance, even though I know I would miss being with him. I still wonder if I am self-inflicting. Greg was not the only man that told me I was hurting myself. Well, I guess one day I will find out.* Every week an appointment was set to see an apartment. Sheaba beat the pavement, making strong efforts to find something nice for her and the children. Finally, the sun shined on her efforts; she got a call to move into a huge single-family home. The house was nice but needed a little bit of rodent control. The owner promised to take care of that after she moved in, so she accepted the home.

Sheaba happily told the children when they got home from school about the new home; they too was excited. She asked that they keep quiet about it; she wanted to tell Greg herself. Before she could tell him, he had come home with an attitude and started an argument because she had not cooked. Surprised, because Greg hated arguing, she tried to brace herself and ignore it. When he began saying hurtful things and demanded she quickly find some place to go, Sheaba cursed at him and yelled to the top of her lungs how much she hated him; then she told him about her new home. She thought he might put her out right then, but he just left the house and did not return until the next morning. Sheaba's heart was broken that he stayed away from home all night, but what could she do? Things had been broken for quite some time.

The next day, Sheaba returned Greg's house keys.

"Where are you going?" he asked.

"Remember? I found a home."

"But I thought the house was not ready yet."

"It is not ready, but I pulled some strings to move in earlier."

He seemed pleased, but when the hired movers arrived and began to remove the bedroom set, he flipped out. Calmly, Sheaba reminded Greg, "I paid for the set, you paid for layaway, step aside or we can get the police involved. I have a receipt that proves what I have said to you and I will win. Your choice." Greg argued for a little while with Sheaba, hoping she would leave the set, but realized she was not giving up; he left her alone about it, and she left in peace.

Sheaba had been out of Greg's house for about five months and was offered a middle-income apartment by the Alabama Housing Authority. Sheaba had no contact with Greg but thought about him a lot. Her accepting the apartment upset her current landlord—he'd put a lot of money into fixing the house as she'd requested—but Sheaba apologized and told him it was the best move for her and the children. Immediately, she packed again, and moved to her new place. The neighborhood was very nice and quiet, different from all the other places she lived on her own.

After she lived there for almost a year, Greg came back into her life. She knew it was not a good idea to return to him, but she did anyway. Greg may not have been good for her emotionally, but financially he was great. He always found a way to support her and the kids, even if it was just buying her groceries. She knew it was wrong to use him that way, but she needed the help. She started falling for him again—he seemed different now, but maybe that was because she no longer lived with him. It was great, but six months into the relationship, they fell out again. Sheaba punched him in the face, and he called the police to have her barred from his place. That was the end of their relationship for a very long time—until she moved again.

Sheaba worked hard to make changes in her life during her time apart from Greg. Working two jobs and going to school kept her mind off Greg, but it caused her to neglect her children. She did the best she could by putting them in summer sport programs and being there when she could. They made friends in the neighborhood, participated in summer activities, and helped Sheaba keep the house clean. Sheaba's hard work paid off; after cleaning up her credit enough to look for a home, she entered the Habitat for Humanity program, completed the one-year journey of building a house, and moved into her newly built home just before Christmas. The first summer in her home, Greg came back again. Sheaba called him to help her with some things around the house; he was the only man that she could call at the time. She did not have a good relationship going with her older siblings and her mother, somehow things changed when she changed. Greg and Sheaba did not get back together but they remained friends. Things were finally moving in the right direction for Sheaba and her children. Shortly, making things a bit more positive, Sheaba dedicated her life to Christ. Being consistent with going to church made her home peaceful and filled her and the children's heart with joy.

The Turning Point

Sheaba's friend Gina invited her to church. The experience was great, as she had never heard the Word so profound. The Pastor not only preached but used analogies and acted out the sermon. It was the first time Sheaba felt what people called the Holy Spirit; her body was exposed to a feeling that made her feel vulnerable. The sermon spoke to her situations, which brought tears to her eyes. She cried out so hard that she embarrassed herself, and she wanted to hide. The followers in the church, however, encouraged her to continue praising and worshiping God. Everyone was so nice and supportive that she joined the church. The Word that was poured out by the preacher showed her that her sufferings were induced by her own weaknesses, self-pity, and lack of knowledge and wisdom. Her world was built around men—getting them to love her and making her feel safe. She totally trusted them with her life. Her hope was as high as the mountains that her past pain would be relieved through them, and they would rescue her from misery. They were used as her god, and while she was with them, the outward pain was erased, but inwardly it was still there.

Because the pain was still there, it was easy for men to push her emotional buttons to bring out the war that laid dormant inside, and the rush of aggression she felt was great. Although she had been taught it was not ladylike to show aggression, the world indicated that it was only right for her to carry on that way. If people hurt her, it was within her rights to do whatever she needed to do to get them to back off. Contrary to what the world believed, the Word of God said in Deuteronomy 32:35, "It is mine to avenge; I will repay. In due time their foot will slip; their day of disaster is near and their doom rushes upon them."

The closer Sheaba got to God, the more she desired to be in a healthy relationship with a man. It was only through God that she recognized she attracted men who mirrored her own behavior. In order to receive God's kings, she had to become one of God's queens. She needed a lot of changes, inside and outside, and only God could do that. Change sounded simple, but in the process of trying to do it, many issues arose. It was a tough, miserable cycle to attack, especially when it seemed as if she was in it alone. Sheaba could taste change, but she could not reach it. Although her life had changed, her old behaviors still haunted her. Her mind was never at peace. To trust someone to love her and respect her was like pulling her own teeth. Many thoughts raced through her mind, good and bad, as she wondered how to be brave enough to stop fighting for herself naturally and allow God to do it for her.

While lost in thought, to her amazement, the presence of God entered into her space and made her feel the way she desired men to make her feel. *How can this be?* she asked herself. He made her feel pretty and desirable. His encouraging words in the Bible showed her how worthy she was to him and made her heart yearn for more of him. He said he died so that she would be made free from bondage; and the chains that held her captive deep inside would fall off. Imprisonment was not made by someone else but by her, as she had made provision to protect herself from the ugliness of the world. Also, she had to protect herself from herself. The person she created when she ran away from home as a teenager was sweet, sly, and vicious. If no one crossed her, she was sweet, but when someone rubbed her the wrong way, she bit harder than a snake.

But God spoke deep into her soul:

> For you formed my inward parts; you knitted me together in my mother's womb. I praise you, for I am fearfully and wonderfully made. Wonderful are your works; my soul knows it very well. My frame was not hidden from you, when I was being made in secret, intricately woven in the depths of the earth. Your eyes saw my unformed

substance; in your book were written, every one of them,
the days that were formed for me, when as yet there was
none of them. (Psalms 139:13–16)

God met her where she was. Being herself was the key to being loved. He never once made her feel as if she needed to be anything more to win his love. While in his presence, he comforted her in every area of sadness. He never lied to her, and he always showed her, in a loving way, when she was wrong. When she was not willing to heed his direction, he would allow her to suffer the consequences, and then he would be there to show love again as he redirected. The pain she felt from his redirection was real, but he never uttered a nasty word. Although he reminded her of from where he brought her, which often reminded her of the pain and suffering, he showed her that he had more for her in the future. He had plans to rebuild her; plans to give her a life filled with love and joy.

He never used her past against her negatively; he used her past to bring her out of bondage. Although she knew God is a Spirit, it felt like she was dating a natural man. *How was it possible that this Spirit connected with her desires?* Sheaba thought. The thought brought a rejuvenated joy to her soul. However, as she settled these thoughts in her mind, her eyes teared up, because her heart was not right toward people in the way God was with her. Conviction policed her past and present evil intentions and actions toward people. It would have been better to have known God in the past in the way she was learning at that moment. Then she would have known how to behave correctly. There never would have been a hand raised toward another but toward God. There would not have been a negative word from her tongue, as she would have yielded it to God. Oh, the pain she felt at that moment, thinking back on all the fights she could have prevented and all the cursing at people she could have kept to herself. God showed her how to love them regardless of the pain they had imposed on her. Sheaba deemed the pain too great to even think about loving someone who had harmed her, and she wondered how God could do it for her and others. It was a deed that no human being could ever handle.

There was no time to think about all of that, however as it would just overwhelm her even more and push her back into yesterday, rather than moving forward to a new day. God was ready to show her how to move into the next realm of life with him—a change that inevitably would be great for her and the children. The time was now; if not, she would forever be stuck in her world of hurt.

Sheaba believed she was ready to totally give her life to Christ, but in the back of her mind, she allowed those questions she fought to hinder her. *Would I be able to commit to God's call and direction? Am I ready to stop seeking men, which is my biggest problem?* After her experience with God, she thought there was no way a man could compete with how he made her feel. Despite what she thought, her body still desired to be touched by a human hand in the way God touched her—but more. Only God had what she needed to be released from the grip of men influences, but Sheaba was hypnotized by coitus, and the addiction was overwhelming. It was a struggle to give that up.

God knew the desires of her heart but pressed upon her his anointed weight to cover her from those evil desires. Sheaba was fighting the wrong fight, and God wanted to teach her how to lean on him and fight her fleshly desires. When she tried fighting her flesh, she would always lose because she failed to include God. Therefore, God allowed her to have the desires of her heart, and that was tearing her apart. Outwardly, she appeared happy and satisfied, but inside, she was tormented.

God could not bear watching her darken her soul any longer, she had fallen into the deep waters of humanistic desires, so whenever she started to drown, he would pull her out. It was not her time to die; he needed her in the kingdom. No matter how many times she betrayed him with a man, she would fall deeper in the depths of the water of her humanistic desires, and God would save her. He heard her cries in the wilderness and comforted her, even when she did not deserve it. God did everything to get her to trust him, but she would give him just a little bit and run away again. No matter how hard Sheaba fought to do what was right by God, it seemed as if unrighteousness was her comfort, while doing good was more unbearable. *How can the war of my flesh be killed if I keep giving in to my weakness?* she thought. God attempted many ways to show her how to work through it; she tried and tried until she moved one step forward in a new direction.

As she made one step, God took multiple steps to lead her to the destiny he planned for her. While she was resting, he would give her dreams and visions of his love, and she would wake up in a great mood, feeling worthy. When she daydreamed, God would show her visions of his love and purpose for her life. At the same time, he would show her warning signs of going back to her old life. Even though she had not totally grown in Christ and had not built a relationship with him, she knew the visions she encountered were not from her own conscience. Her intuition was good but not as clear as God's visions. As she believed in God, she knew those visions would prove to be real and would be carried out just as she had seen them. Although it appeared as if Sheaba did not want to give up her evil desires, God knew she truly had a strong desire to rid them.

The strongholds in Sheaba's life were vicious, which was why she had been overcome by her addiction. She was amazed by God's strength in her life, which helped her move out of suffering and gave her a greater push to fight her lustful desires. Nevertheless, there was always something that forced her to see things differently. Those evil desires had her mind twisted to believe that because God was a Spirit, he could never apply the physical passion that man could.

Immediately, God dropped a stunning word in her heart: "Do not conform to the pattern of this world, but be transformed by the renewing of your mind. Then you will be able to test and approve what God's will is, his good, pleasing and perfect will" (Romans 12:2 NIV). Sheaba did not read the Bible often, but when God dropped scriptures in her heart, she would run and grab it to see what God had to say, and those words resonated within her greatly. While Sheaba did not know how to renew her mind, as it was full of old stuff, she wondered what steps to take to do it. Through prayer, she asked God to show her how to renew her mind. It was not until she went back to church that she received the answer. The preacher touched on it very well, and again, Sheaba found herself crying, as if she had lost a loved one. It was always overwhelming to cry at church like that. The people at church never made her feel bad about praising God in a loud cry; they knew she was experiencing the overwhelming presence of God.

The encounters with God were sobering. It was amazing how God would respond to her in many ways. If she asked God for something, and he did not respond to her consciousness, he would respond through a word from the pastor, or television, or a stranger on the street. It was always surprising but rewarding and right on time. Loving God was a beautiful thing, but it was still hard to untangle herself from the web of men. The truth was that God was her Savior, and men were her enemy. Men were the reason she kept falling into the deep waters of her dark soul, where she had no treading experience and was likely to drown. She had to make a choice, and she had to make it fast, or she would drown and never experience a true life of love and the peace of God.

Sheaba always blamed men for her position, as she hated them. It was not all men's fault that she experienced such a horrible childhood. But in her mind, they always manipulated and mistreated her. She knew her decisions were partly to blame, but she never took full responsibility for them; her hard head often sent her back into the deep waters of her dark soul. Every time she succumbed to her emotions, and desires, she would nearly drown. It was evident that God's love allowed her to experience the depth of the water in increments, as he knew how much she could take. She was self-abased with just a little bit of faith. She repeated the deep-water cycle until she got tired of potentially drowning, and she acknowledged the presence of God. The very last time God rescued her, he allowed her to go so deep into the water that it appeared bottomless. While she was immersed (in her mess), her mind honed in on the love of God and his mercy. Feeling the conviction of God was disappointing, and defying him for men was hurtful. Stress overwhelmed her, and her legs weakened. Everything appeared dark, and she felt her body temperature rise, as if she were in a sauna. God met her where she was, pulled her out of the deep waters of her miserable dark soul, and breathed life into her lungs.

In the process of regaining consciousness, she panted heavily and coughed repeatedly, and tears flowed down her cheeks. In fear, she immediately opened her mouth to praise the only man who had ever loved her. In that moment, she believed that God was truly real, and he had come to spare and save her life. He could have allowed her to die in her sins, "But God, who is rich in mercy, for his great love wherewith he loved us, even when we were dead in sins, hath quickened us together with Christ (by grace ye are saved)" (Ephesians 2:4–5 KJV).

God's power, which was aggressively exposing, uprooting, and purging her from her past, created a stench that seeped through her pores. But when God finished with her, a sweet-smelling perfume replaced it that pleased Him. Each time she encountered the presence and power of God, there was a shift in her body that jolted her flesh and forced it to surrender to him. *Why didn't he let me die? My life is too painful to overcome, and happiness would never find me. Why was it so hard to believe there was hope and to believe that God deemed me worthy?* she thought. The questions in her mind kept coming, but she interrupted them by speaking to her flesh: "If I don't let go of my past, I will be married to it!" *That was powerful! Beyond my comprehension. Those words did not come from me, so they had to have come from the Lord.* she thought.

God was the only way she could divorce her past and be healed. Sheaba wanted to be married but not to her past. Sheaba thought, *My past is so deeply rooted and dark that it would take forever to win the divorce case.* Seeking Christ was her ticket to change, but it was a battle because it required commitment. Sheaba was never committed to anything but her own desires. Starting with prayer as her first commitment helped her tremendously. She believed that prayer changed things and put her on the right track to be committed to changing her life. As she lifted her hands in surrender and lifted her voice, she could feel the warmth of God's blood running through her veins.

"God grant me the opportunity to change my life from the strongholds of my past! Teach me your ways, and show me how to take steps in your direction! I am a sinner, and I have no clue how to live in this life. Help me to be more like you and be committed to the things of you."

I don't know what I'm getting myself into, she thought, *but it can't be any worse than what I've gone through in my past.* The more Sheaba acknowledged her sins, the more God told her about herself and prepped her for change. The process was a bit much; it took more effort than she had imagined. It was important, however, that she stay the course to keep the vinegar's bitterness from the belly of her soul. Every time she thought of connecting with her past, God would remind her of the deep waters and how he had kept it from collapsing her lungs.

The closer she got to winning the divorce, the harder the devil fought to keep her where she was. It did not take much for her flesh to experience a percussive flare. Desires and emotions were a beast to fight, so she sought God for his protection and for covering over her mind. Studying the Bible more gave her insight on things she had never understood, and her perspective on life changed little by little. Her understanding of the content of the Bible was ravishingly appetizing. She did not want to become overly zealous, but she sought God to gain understanding of the works of her flesh. In her devotion time, he gave her this:

> But I see another law at work in me, waging war against
> the law of my mind and making me a prisoner of the law
> of sin at work within me. (Romans 7:23 NIV)

> For I know that good itself does not dwell in me, that it
> is in my sinful nature. For I have the desire to do what is
> good, but I cannot carry it out. (Romans 7:18 NIV)

Sheaba was a risk-taker, at times indirectly. While trying to allow the scriptures to resonate within her, she would indirectly play games with the ungodly spirits of desire and emotion. Those familiar spirits often caught her unaware. In the process of learning and growing in God, the enemy had his way of flaring her flesh to capacity to where she would fall. God raised the bar and began a deep uprooting, as he knew Sheaba, and he refused to allow her past to become her foundation.

This time as Sheaba went into prayer, it was a bit stronger than before. It was more than prayer; it was worship. She recognized the difference because she was no longer on her knees or sprawled out on the floor. She found herself waving her hands in the air and dancing around, often leaping, and swaying across the floor. Visions crossed her eyes as they were closed; her mind was in tune with the voice of God. It was overwhelming but comforting this time, and God spoke: "Regard not them that have familiar spirits; neither seek after wizards, to be defiled by them; I am the Lord your God" (Leviticus 19:31).

After coming out of worship, she tried to understand what God was saying. Reading it over and over, she waited for God to reveal understanding of his Word. Taking the initiative, she researched *familiar spirits*, and this is what she found: sorcerers had spirits as their servants, ready to obey their commands. Sheaba understood that emotions and desires were the evilness of Satan, attempting to lead her back into the depth of the waters. Those spirits could smell the stench of her sinfulness and entertained every aspect of it. It was in that moment that Sheaba chose to close herself off to men. She ceased going out to clubs, dressing provocatively, and surrounding herself with people who tempted her to indulge in things of her past.

God replaced all that she gave up with seasoned prayer warriors—spiritual friends who showed her a good time. Sheaba's children found new friends in the church and became grounded and rooted more than she. She became a praise leader and a Sunday school teacher, and she helped wherever she could in the church. It felt really good to breathe in a different environment, and she hoped that she would never go back to her old life.

In Sheaba's time of solitude, away from her spiritual family, she still had thoughts of never experiencing true love from a man. She loved her life with Christ and her newfound friends, but her inner self desired and hoped for a relationship. Her lack of faith blinded her to relational hope, and her heart gave up on the idea of healthy relationships. She understood that natural relationships were more familiar than spiritual. Because she did not have a full understanding of how to balance the two, she struggled with controlling her thoughts when her heart longed for a husband. It hurt deep within when she felt as if she would never experience the love of marriage with man as she experienced love with God.

As she served God, she did not consider it as being in a relationship with him because she did not know what is was like to be in a real relationship. It felt like she was going through the motions with God—doing the right thing to head in the right direction, but she was not sure. Leaving her thoughts of a possible relationship with God, she began remembering her pathetic life, when she was always sad and feeling down before she met Christ. There was never a thought that her life would be anything but what it was—shameful, dirty, and rejected. "But God!"

Sheaba, being the fighter she was, spoke to herself: "I must get up and fight! I will not go back by allowing my thoughts to send me into depression. I am a winner. I will win this battle! I am a child of God, and with him. I will overcome!" Again, with more effort than before, the fight was on. Using the little strength she possessed, she paced the floor of her living room aggressively, and shouted, "I need to learn more about who I am! I want to look at myself differently! I want to love myself!" She screamed even louder, "What do I need to do, God! Who am I? I will no longer be who they say I am! Fix me!"

Tears of pain streamed down her face. Her chest felt as if there were weights upon it. Her head throbbed, and she slid to the floor. Lying prostrate, she silenced herself, hoping to hear from God. Unfortunately, there were no words from him, no sound except the air. Everything stood still, her mind was clear, and the peace of God put her to sleep right there on the floor of her living room. She needed the rest, she was exhausted from the prayer and overthinking things.

CHAPTER 3

God's Relational Therapy

After Sheaba's outburst to God, she was content. God laid his hand on her body and thrust peace upon it. Rest and relaxation was bad words to her body; all she ever had experienced was stress and depression. She always had been on edge and tense about something.

When she finally opened her eyes, everything looked bright. The sun was peeking through the living room blinds, and peace was still in the room. The illuminating sun always confirmed that God was pleased with her, as did the sweet melody of a bird singing. She remained on the floor for a minute to adjust her focus and thanked God for his presence. As she stood up, her body felt light. In that moment, she was no longer bogged down with the weight of her past, and she felt like a new woman.

She began cleaning her house to get rid of the residue of what had been released from her and into the atmosphere. She played good gospel music as she cleaned. She danced and sang until her work was done. For a moment, happiness was upon her, but in the back of her mind, she knew the weight of her past would return. She made a valiant effort not to focus on her past, as it was beneficial to instead focus on getting through the purging and uprooting process. Her desire was to allow God to rid her of generational curses and all other internal negatives. In that process, she hoped to see a greater progression in her life and walk with God.

Trusting God while walking with him was hard for Sheaba. She understood that progression in life would come through him. In her past, she had trusted many others, but they later had deceived her. She forgave them and had no hard feelings toward them; she endured the pain and moved on. Unlike her trust with God, she would become weak in her body and lose faith. She hoped God would forgive her, and she got into his presence, which was her comfort, and basked in him until she was at ease. She wished she could stay there and never leave, but she often was hindered by her emotions. The issues she faced caused her to believe things would never get better. In her self-pity, she wondered, *what is the purpose of trusting God—and how is it done?* Even though God did not answer her questions, she thought positively and refused to accept that trusting God was a hard task. The desire to trust God produced a greater strength to hear him and follow his instructions. Sheaba had endured a lot of pain in her life and believed that God had helped her thus far; therefore, it didn't hurt to learn to trust him and endure the pain of doing so.

Sheaba learned that trusting God meant to deny her truth and accept his. In her walk with God, she had to let go of her way of doing things—let go of her typical resolutions to issues, her natural way of seeing life, and the way she heard things. Knowing this, she realized that she would build a deeper relationship with God if she trusted him. Sheaba thought, *If I can accomplish this task, then maybe some of the miracles of healing and the abundant blessings in the Bible will come to pass in my life.*

She fought hard to keep her mind on God and trust him. She consistently studied scriptures in the Bible that spoke of trust. She attended church regularly and surrounded herself with people who not only believed God but had great godly faith and trust. She needed to know what his miracles looked like in others so that her application would not seem false. Sheaba's friend Gina, who had won her to Christ, stood by her side and answered as many questions as she could to assist her with her quest. *She is great!* Sheaba thought. *She always explains things so thoroughly and backs them up with valid scriptures.* Yet it was hard to retain everything she learned. It was a blessing that the pastor of their church was very good with acting out his sermons, because it helped Sheaba retain some things, but his sermons didn't always touch on *trust*.

To learn more about trust, Sheaba created her own trust study and devotion. Barnes & Noble and Amazon had the best selection of books on trust, and she researched the internet on trusting God. One scripture passage, in particular, opened Sheaba's eyes and heart: 2 Kings 5:13–15. Naaman's servant asked a simple question: "If the prophet had told you to do some great thing, would you not have done it? How much more, when he tells you, 'Wash and be cleansed!'"

Trust sounded like a simple thing—God was asking Sheaba to do as he commanded. *Why is it so hard to do?* Sheaba thought. She understood in her heart that flesh was naturally disobedient to the things of God, especially those that did not seem real or attainable. God often spoke to her about her flesh when it was out of alignment with his word. At times, his word confounded her carnal mind. The more Sheaba began to grasp the concept of trusting God, the more she questioned herself. She thought, *How can I be so stubborn? How can I ask God for something and expect him to do it, when I can't do something so simple for Him?* Sheaba's heart was broken, yet it took a long time for her to completely trust God. She would trust at times, but then at other times, she would allow fear to keep her from God's instructions. She came to realize that when she faced troubles that overburdened her heart, doing things her own way made her a winner for only a moment. When God called to her, he gave instructions and directions, and acknowledged to her that anything that was done contrary to them would fail.

Sheaba set high standards for herself in an attempt to consistently trust God, but she was not always successful. Every day, even when fighting on her knees, the battle within her flesh did not stop, but she could feel her emotions and desire being checked by God's word. Sheaba's fleshy desires consistently overruled her spirit within, and the strongholds of life had her bound. The strongholds of her life were familiar, and at times it felt good to stay there, rather than to resist being there. However, the consequences of entertaining those familiar spirits hurt beyond measure. *There has to be a way to bring my flesh under God's authority,* she thought. She grabbed her Bible to look up scriptures about her flesh, and one stood out: "For the flesh lusteth against the Spirit, and the Spirit against the flesh: and these are contrary the one to the other: so that ye cannot do the things that ye would" (Galatians 5:17 KJV).

Wow, she thought, *my body and spirit fight with each other? So does trusting God become a battle?* Spiritual warfare—the hindrance to trusting God—was trying to become a winner in her body. That explained why at times, when she believed she was on track with doing things the godly way, she would fail. She wondered if it was spiritual warfare when she experienced demonic spirit encounters during her resting periods. Evil spirits would attack when she was vulnerable, paralyzing her body and restricting her voice through dreams or causing her to feel delirious. The first time it happened, Sheaba was filled with overwhelming fear, as she did not know what to do. Someone told her that if it happened again, she should plead the blood of Jesus against the spirit; she did it, and—surprisingly—it worked. That gave her confidence every time it happened. Each time, the demonic spirit would be stronger than the last, and fear would return, preventing her from breaking its hold, and it would last longer.

Sheaba later sought God for his divine protection. He had protected her before she knew him, so she believed he was still doing it. Finally, when the enemy attacked again, she found a better way to beat him. When he took her voice, she would pray in her conscious, *I bind you, devil, in the name of Jesus. Release me and go back from whence you have come!* Immediately, the spirit of the enemy would release her.

Sheaba was ecstatic at the defeat of the enemy through God, which began to show that she started trusting that he would fight on her behalf. This was her first step of trust, but now she had to be consistent so she could beat what she called her pathetic life.

Sheaba faithfully stayed before God, participated in random church fasts, read, and prayed, all of which allowed Sheaba to become closer to God and learn new things about herself and the life she lived. Her strength was greater than before, and she was no longer easily angered or frustrated. Although she learned negative things about herself while reading the bible, her grieving moments turned into appreciation, because it inspired her to do much better. As she continued reading the bible, she understood what she was reading more and more. Reading made her more aware of the devils tactics. Despite her awareness, she still had a hard time resisting the temptations that were before her. Because her flesh was weak, she would desire things that were against the word of God. Sheaba's spiritual awareness was not strong enough to recognize all the evil plans lurking in her presence, so he would attack her when she was most vulnerable; for example; when she was sleeping or when she was in a sad state of mind. In this instance, God stepped in for her and fought on her behalf.

> For we wrestle not against flesh and blood, but against principalities, against powers, against the rulers of the darkness of this world, against spiritual wickedness in high places. (Ephesians 6:12 KJV)

The fear in knowing the enemy had that much power over the flesh made Sheaba fight that much harder to get closer to God. Sheaba was a fighter and did not mind raising her fist to protect herself and her territory. She did not care how big or how tough the individuals were; she would stand up like a soldier. The devil always smelled fear and tried to cause her to flinch, but she never backed down.

Ephesians 6:12 showed her how much she needed God's consistent protection—protection from those things she couldn't see, hear, feel, or touch. She no longer only prayed before going to bed at night; she developed the ability to pray when she got up in the morning and throughout the day. Her precautions were beneficial, as they covered her weaknesses. She learned that whenever she became lackadaisical in her prayer life, she would succumb to unclean spirits, especially those familiar lustful ones. Sheaba knew the enemy paid close attention to her actions and would always impose upon them fairly quickly. He loved her fighting spirit, the one that was violent and vehement, so the harder she sought God, the harder he attacked.

While Sheaba fought through her fear of the unseen spirits, she still tried to trust God in all things. Except when God would expose to her to the truth about herself. It wasn't easy to accept what God thought of her as a person, especially when she thought she was a good person. Feeling pitiful, she waited on God to answer her deepest question: *Why do things happen the way they do in my life?* God took his time with responding, as he knew she was not ready for the answer. Her pride would not allow her to accept his truth. She was sure to relapse in anger, and without understanding, she would run into the arms of evil. Even though she had not received a response from God, she was determined to walk strong in him. She constantly reminded herself of her pathetic life before God. It was redundant, but as she continued to remember her pathetic life, it helped her realize why she was making efforts to trust God for a significant change to her life.

When Sheaba prayed, she would always listen for an answer from God – Instead, he showed her visions of the journey he had been taking her through. Sheaba considered it to be a therapeutic journey, one that was not quite pleasant, but memorable. The journey had been filled with spiritual battles that sifted more energy than she could imagine from her body. Sheaba thought, *Though it was hard, it was worth it.*

Sheaba still fighting to control her evil and sometimes selfish thoughts failed. Her natural thoughts blinded her spiritual vision. Sheaba thought, *how do I deny my natural vision for the spiritual vision?* Finally, she understood how her natural conscience could be in conflict with the spiritual —she could hear the negative and the positive going back and forth in her mind as if there were two people arguing. The war between her carnal mind and her spiritual mind induced headaches and chest pains that were so heavy that it caused weakness. It was totally impossible for Sheaba to fight her battles alone, she needed God to do it for her. Sheaba had always fought her own battles, so it was not easy to accept that God had to fight her battles. She'd won those physical battles in her past almost every time, but she'd lost her worth and the respect of those she battled against. In those times, she could care less, because she believed she had nothing to lose.

When Sheaba learned that the battles of life she was attempting to fight on her own were not hers to fight but God's, she recognized she had never won those personal battles. Sheaba thought, *my fight was in vain, which is why I felt such great agony afterwards. I thought I was supposed to fight for myself when others come against me. Now I know that my fight is limited and when God fight for me, I win. Amazing!* Sheaba had an innate ability to be a self-protector; it was not that she wanted to remain that way, but it was the only way to prove her independence to her oppressors. She tried giving her battles to God, but her lack of patience caused humiliation. Her oppressor was always man. She hated the very thought of a man dominating her, so she worked out at the gym, to compete with their strength. It was a matter of time that she would have to physically war with a man and she wanted to be prepared; losing was not an option. That attitude began in her past when she was in physical abusive relationships. But, she understood, it was time to hang up her boxing gloves, let God fight, and allow her oppressors to believe they had won against her.

In reality a loss was a win in God's eyes. When God fought on her behalf, he was fighting inside of her, and her oppressors felt his wrath. Her oppressors were familiar with her combative, aggressive behavior, but she hit them with humility. Her humility to them was weakness, so they tried harder to push her, but they only became desperately angry. It was all new and awkward to Sheaba, and surely her flesh desired to flare up and fight, but she kept it under the subjection of God's power. Sheaba learned in that moment that she could walk away with a win because she gave her battles to God.

> For the word of God is quick, and powerful, sharper than any two-edged sword, piercing even to the dividing asunder of soul and spirit, and unto the joints and marrow, and is a discerner of the thoughts, and intent of the heart.
> (Hebrews 4:12 KJV)

The word of God was true, her oppressors were cut by the words that God gave her to fight, and it cut them deeper than a knife, so much so that it caused their anger to heighten while trying to lift hers. Sheaba was grateful that God knew her thoughts and the intent of her heart, therefore, he fought for her at the right time.

Sheaba loved her personal contact with God, having his undivided attention always moved her to tears of conviction and joy. Although Sheaba continued to struggle in her walk with God, she would still feel the various types of lust, anger, and aggression haunting her. The battle within was atrocious. Sheaba thought, *I did not realize how deep those feelings and emotions were inside.* She prayed and prayed, but constantly repenting was getting old. Sheaba wanted to give up, she thought, *why am I constantly trying to do something I obviously cannot do? I am not committed enough to walk with God.* Those negative thoughts developed after she read the scripture in Jeremiah 15:6—I am tired of always giving you another chance. (NLT).

He did not stop there. One time, she painfully went deep into prayer before God about her undeniable sexual desires. While she was praying, she could hear in her conscious that she should repent about those desires, but she refused to speak them out loud. It was not something she was ready to totally give up. She cried so long and hard, that her tears created a puddle on her living room floor.

God whispered a scripture in her ear, and she immediately raised herself from the floor and grabbed her Bible to read it. Frantically flipping through the pages of the Bible, she was anxious to read the good news that he had always provided. Unfortunately, anticipated joy turned into sorrow when she read this:

> Upon a high and lofty mountain, you have made your bed. You also went up there to offer sacrifice. Behind the door and the door post you have set up your sign; indeed, far removed from me, you have uncovered yourself, and have gone up and made your bed wide. And you have made an agreement for yourself with them, you have loved their bed, you have looked on their manhood. You

have journeyed to the king with oil and increased your perfumes; you have sent your envoys a great distance and made them go down to Sheol (land of the dead). (Isaiah 57:7–9 NASB)

It was important to God that Sheaba understand how he viewed her behavior. He certainly was not trying to humiliate her but his words were definitely meant to chastise. He needed her to release her opiate addiction, which was coitus, to him, so he could wash her clean.

Shocked at God's response, she was offended and put the book down. She sat on the floor, disappointed with what she had read. She often highlighted and dated what the Lord had spoken to her in the Bible, but this time she refused. The root of Sheaba's problem was her opiate addiction (coitus with men), the one thing that she used to ease her troubled mind. God was attacking her issues from the root. Sheaba understood from that scripture, that if she continued with her addiction, her spirituality would face the penalty of death. However, God did not put her through therapy to fail, his goal was always to chastise to bring her back to him.

Despite Sheaba's disappointment, she knew that addiction was alive inside, but she did not expect God to expose her so abruptly. It was difficult for Sheaba to give up that addiction; it seemed like the more she tried to stay away from men, the more she was driven to them. Later down the line, when she attempted to testify to the encounter with God, she was hindered because she hadn't highlighted the scripture in her Bible to back up her testimony. That was her first lesson in learning never to go before God in partiality. He exposed her thoughts publicly to let her know he heard what she was afraid to say and pray.

That hard lesson caused her to think, *every time I go before God in prayer, and regardless of the chastisement of his Word, I will always record it for future testimonies. His Word says we overcome by the word of our testimonies.*

And they have defeated him by the blood of the lamb and by their testimony. And they did not love their lives so much that they were afraid to die. (Revelation 12:11 NLT)

In this part of therapy, she learned to take heed, wait for instructions, and follow him, rather than hide and run.

But do not just listen to God's word. You must do what it says. Otherwise, you are only fooling yourselves. (James 1:22 NLT)

Though Sheaba recognized that Isaiah 57:7-9 was true exposure, it took years for her to accept it. Had she accepted it sooner, she would have applied it to her life and made provision to move past it. The stronghold that kept her in bondage brought many challenges and embarrassment to her walk with Christ because, much like an actual substance drug addiction, so was her lust for men. Therefore, God spoke another hard word to her, years later.

> Just try to find one hilltop where you haven't gone to worship other gods by having sex. You sat beside the road like a robber in ambush except you offered yourself to every passerby. Your sins of unfaithfulness have polluted the land. So, the Lord, refused to let the spring rains fall. But just like a prostitute, you still have no shame for what you have done. You call me your father or your long-lost friend; you beg me to stop being angry, but you won't stop sinning. (Jeremiah 3:2–7 CEV)

He was right; Sheaba was not ashamed, as she still loved the attention from men and how they put out her torch with their opium. Although God spoke a harsh word—it was chastisement, even though Sheaba took it the first time as cruel—she was grateful the second time because even though he had grown weary of her repentance, she recognized he still had not given up on her.

It was evident that God saw how her story would end if she did not kick her addiction. Whenever those urges presented itself, she would go to God. It made her feel better because at least she was being truthful in prayer. In her prayers, rather than tell God she didn't want to be addicted to lust for men, she proclaimed she wanted to be addicted. It was true! She really believed she did not want to give it up, because she always did the opposite of what God spoke to her while in prayer. It was her way of facing the truth about herself in hopes that she could see the hand of God work in her situation. At times he created roadblocks to prevent her from moving forward with her disobedient plans. But, there were times she pushed pass them.

Again, during her devotional time, God approached her about his disapproval of her addiction through reading the first chapter of the book of Isaiah. The entire chapter had weighty detail that convicted her soul. As she read it in its entirety, she understood God was giving her an ultimatum, coupled with a bit of anger and love. She felt like he was threatening her soul salvation to get her to face the truth and allow him to deliver her from what he considered illicit behavior. He wanted to give her the desires of her heart the right way, without the addiction, but she could not let it go.

A Rebellious Nation

Hear me, you heavens! Listen, earth! For the LORD has spoken: "I reared children and brought them up, but they have rebelled against me. The ox knows its master, he knoweth his owner's manger, but Israel does not know, my people do not understand." Woe to the sinful nation, a people whose guilt is great, a brood of evildoers, children given to corruption! They have forsaken the LORD; they have spurned the Holy One of Israel and turned their backs on him.

Why should you be beaten anymore? Why do you persist in rebellion? Your whole head is injured, your whole heart afflicted. From the sole of your foot to the top of your head there is no soundness—only wounds and welts and open sores, not cleansed or bandaged or soothed with olive oil. Your country is desolate, your cities burned with fire; your fields are being stripped by foreigners right before you, laid waste as when overthrown by strangers. Daughter of Zion is left like a shelter in a vineyard, like a hut in a cucumber field, like a city under siege. Unless the LORD Almighty had left us some survivors, we would have become like Sodom, we would have been like Gomorrah.

Hear the word of the LORD, you rulers of Sodom; listen to the instruction of our God, you people of Gomorrah! "The multitude of your sacrifices—what are they to me?" says the LORD. "I have more than enough of burnt offerings, of rams and the fat of fattened animals; I have no pleasure in the blood of bulls and lambs and goats. When you come to appear before me, who has asked this of you, this trampling of my courts? Stop bringing meaningless offerings! Your incense is detestable to me. New Moons, Sabbaths and convocations—I cannot bear your worthless assemblies. Your New Moon feasts and your appointed festivals I hate with all my being. They have become a burden to me; I am weary of bearing them. When you spread out your hands in prayer, I hide my eyes from you; even when you offer many prayers, I am not listening. Your hands are full of blood!

Wash and make yourselves clean. Take your evil deeds out of my sight; stop doing wrong. Learn to do right; seek justice. Defend the oppressed. Take up the cause of the fatherless; plead the case of the widow. "Come now, let us settle the matter," says the LORD. "Though your sins are like scarlet, they shall be as white as snow; though they are red as crimson, they shall be like wool. If you are willing and obedient, you will eat the good things of the land; but if you resist and rebel, you will be devoured by the sword." For the mouth of the LORD has spoken.

See how the faithful city has become a prostitute! She once was full of justice; righteousness used to dwell in her—but now murderers! Your silver has become dross, your choice wine is diluted with water. Your rulers are rebels, partners with thieves; they all love bribes and chase after gifts. They do not defend the cause of the fatherless; the widow's case does not come before them. Therefore the Lord, the LORD Almighty, the Mighty One of Israel, declares: "Ah! I will vent my wrath on my foes and avenge

myself on my enemies. I will turn my hand against you;
I will thoroughly purge away your dross and remove all
your impurities. I will restore your leaders as in days of
old, your rulers as at the beginning. Afterward you will
be called the City of Righteousness, the Faithful City."

Zion will be delivered with justice, her penitent ones
with righteousness. But rebels and sinners will both be
broken, and those who forsake the LORD will perish. "You
will be ashamed because of the sacred oaks in which you
have delighted; you will be disgraced because of the
gardens that you have chosen. You will be like an oak with
fading leaves, like a garden without water. The mighty
man will become tinder and his work a spark; both will
burn together, with no one to quench the fire." (Isaiah
1:2–31 NIV)

What a powerful and disheartening word, Sheaba thought. God's
chastening in the beginning, his love in the middle, and warnings in
the end appealed a stronger conviction than the first and the second
time. God knew she was damaged goods; he understood where she
was in her life and how she got there. He was very direct and wanted
Sheaba to understand what he was feeling after attempting to show
much love, and after providing a loving chastisement. How much
more should he chastise when it served no purpose? He did not want
to remove his hands from Sheaba's life, but if she refused to adhere
to his Word, facing the world alone would surely kill her slowly.

Sheaba wept so hard that when she was done praying, her body
was as sore as if she had been lifting heavy weights. His Word
penetrated her flesh, into the depth of her soul and slaughtered those
hidden agendas. His Word had cut so deep that she had no choice
but to deal with her addiction the hard way—cold turkey. She always
felt inadequate and afraid, so she did not believe she would succeed,
which ultimately would send her back to her addiction. Sheaba's love
for God was genuine, but her consistency in lustful acts did not prove
it very much. Life itself was so hard that it was easier to revert to
what felt comfortable.

Years prior to her desire to change, she would hear other Christians say it was a sin to go to the movies, that drinking was not of God, that going to the gym was not of God, and more. What, then, was life about if those things were not acceptable to God? Sheaba studied and learned that many scriptures referenced those areas. God was very specific about drinking, having entertainment, and health. An overindulgence in drinking caused sin, so that was forbidden if it could not be done in moderation. God was all for being healthy, but if working out took the place of time spent with him, it was unacceptable. Entertainment was fine, as long as it did not harm the spirit, such as with provocative and profane actions.

Sheaba understood that God desired her to enjoy life, but based on her baggage, there were things from which she needed to refrain. Eventually, she learned to work out her own salvation with fear and trembling, rather than accepting someone else's interpretation or looking at others lifestyle and judging their salvation. It was more important to focus on getting her life right with God. Most of all, to be able to balance her natural life with her spiritual life would help her to fulfill a joyful and fruitful lifestyle.

> What is the best thing to do in the short life that God has given us? I think we should enjoy eating, drinking, and working hard. This is what God intends for us to do. Suppose you are very rich and able to enjoy everything you own. Then go ahead and enjoy working hard—this is God's gift to you. God will keep you so happy that you won't have time to worry about each day. (Ecclesiastes 5:18–20 CEV)

The fear Sheaba had in her heart toward God forced her to want to do right by him. Attending church and hearing the Word of God was not enough to sustain her. She had to live the life he predestined for her and allow him to search and judge her through his Word. It was easy listening to the Word that was preached but hard to apply it and carry it out. Surrendering to God and dying to her emotions was a terrible fight. Though she experienced his convictions, the flesh would overrule, and she had no way of knowing how to stop it. It appeared that no one cared to show her, and she did not care to ask. Everyone seemed to be doing their own thing, so she learned the hard way. Those who attempted to teach her to walk the walk were not honestly living in the truth of God themselves. In her blindness, God would allow her to see who they were, openly, and that hurt because she trusted their guidance.

Nevertheless, God never ceased being in her corner to push her in the right direction. In her honesty, God worked with her, and she drove herself farther and farther away from what was true about her addiction. It was evident that God desired Sheaba to come before him in spirit and truth, because every time she went before him in prayer in honesty about her deepest desires, he would show himself to her in various ways. Sometimes he would jog her memory to remind her of the pain she felt when she would indulge in her addiction, while other times he would cause distraction to take her mind from it.

In Sheaba's attempt to go cold turkey from her coitus addiction, she gradually made efforts to research the Bible for scriptures to help. God must have had a plan, as he had already chastised her through his words. He was well aware that she loved coitus more than him, and she was not giving it up any time soon. Coitus was her drug and god; without them, she was miserably depressed. In the back of her mind, the desire to let them go was real this time, but it still hurt to give them up. They were the healing to her pains, and she did not know how to substitute her drug for God. The withdrawal pains were so unbearable, and she could feel her body going through warfare.

A full two weeks had gone by and Sheaba was excited that she had accomplished denouncing her addiction. That was not normal, her addiction was attended to at least two or three times per week. *I am on my way!* she thought. Almost immediately the devils temptation started a fire. He ordered a phone call to her from one of her pushers. When she saw the number on her caller ID, she knew immediately it was a temptation. She struggled not to answer, but she knew he would keep calling until she did, so she answered. The sound of his voice penetrated her body and a hot sensation introduced a light sweat. During the hour of conversation, she put up her best fight to kill her desire to give in. Sheaba had a false hope that if she continue the relationship with her pusher, that one day they will marry. All her pusher was interested in was introducing to her his opium. Every time Sheaba allowed him to inject her with his opium, she would relapse, but she could not resist the taste.

Sheaba's mind was racing, playing visions of a passionate release and then switched to thoughts of the detriment it could cause to her process of change. Unfortunately, her flesh succumbed in its desperation, but while she was on the way to the pusher's house, God immediately spoke to her conscience, showing visions of her past as she drove to her destination. God's still small voice spoke very softly, warning that if she moved forward, she would feel worse than she had after her childhood encounter. God stayed with her while reminding her that her opium addiction came from her childhood and that she did not have to go back down that road.

Her mind was racing much faster than before, which shifted her into an emotional overdrive. Defiantly, she continued the journey to her pusher, totally ignoring the twisted feeling in the pit of her stomach. Somehow along the way, the taste for the drug left her body. She could not understand how or why that suddenly happened; because for the entire ride, her desire to taste the goodness of the drug was extraordinarily overwhelming. Regardless, she forced herself to keep moving.

When she arrived, she wasted no time in getting out of the car and to the door of her pusher. She rang the doorbell, the door opened, and she stepped through the door of defeat. God had been right; she walked in emotionless and walked out emotionally humiliated. After engaging with her pusher, she felt debased. Her self-worth was destroyed, her integrity lost, and the little self-esteem she had was gone. Before her pusher introduced her to his drug, she explained her encounter with God on her way to him, hoping he would refuse to move forward with the plan. She thought he would care because he went to church every Sunday. He even had a Bible on his nightstand, as her father did when he committed incest. Her soul was convicted, and she felt like God left her side. *God! Did you harden my pusher's heart? I know I was disobedient, but he was so mean and selfish toward me. He was not sensitive as he had been in the past. All he wanted to do is handle the business.* Sheaba thought. Sheaba broke through God's barriers of protection and knew she had made the biggest mistake and because of that fear set in.

After her pusher injected her with the opiate drug, he asked, "would you lie here for a while and rest with me?" Sheaba thought, *this man is as messed up as I am. He does not love me, but he wants me to believe that. I do not believe he know love. He read the bible, he goes to church, why did he still partake in the sin?* In Sheaba's conviction, on top of all the humility she felt, without answering, she ran out of her pusher's house as if she were running for her life. He did not run after her, nor did he call to find out what was wrong, or if she was ok. She heard the door shut and lock as she made it to her car, and that hurt worse. *How can he be so insensitive?* she thought.

While heading home, her mind played back the scenario from beginning to end, over and over again, until she burst into a loud wail. The drive home was horrible, so much so that she had to pull over and gather herself to prevent a car accident.

The enemy thought he had won, but Sheaba's convictions saved her from his deadly game. The enemy saw her pain as a victory and plotted to push her into a depression that would end her life by her own hand. Sheaba fooled him; she went home and did the opposite of what he expected. While sitting in the car, she thought about that horrible feeling and was determined to never doubt or overrule the voice and instructions of the Lord again. The valuable lesson she learned opened her thoughts to a new understanding of God and his consistent love for her. Although she desired the things of the world more than God, he loved her more than she realized, and he showed it.

God proved to know everything about her, inside out, through personal encounters and through his Word in the Bible. He knew her deepest desire was not to run to her pusher, she had worked hard at change. Her ignorance to resist the devil led her to her pusher. In God's sovereignty, he showed love toward her. Committed to changing, she aimed to get back on track. Sheaba yelled, "THIS ADDICTION HAS TO STOP!"

Sheaba never forgot that experience, and for the first time in her life, she felt like someone cared about her feelings. It was amazing that this invisible God had shown so much love, despite her disobedience. How could she not serve him? God blatantly exposed her vulnerability, through allowing the enemy to tempt her, he wanted to show the importance of keeping her temple clean. Yet time and time again, she would give in to her lust. Therefore, God removed his hands, and in love, allowed her to do what she wanted. *Why would he do that?* she thought.

Through the love of God, her eyes were opened to the lack of love and regard for her life; she hated herself. When she got home from visiting her pusher that night, she walked into her living room and sat on the couch. After a minute, she began talking aimlessly to herself, beating herself up about what she had done. Her flesh was satisfied, but her body and mind were out of sync with God. Again, she burst into tears, feeling self-pity, wondering how she could get her life back on track after what she had done. She looked up at the ceiling and opened her mouth to talk with God about her addiction and relationships with men. She no longer wanted to wallow in pity but to stand up in the strength of God and face the facts about her behaviors.

Her questions were no longer about why her relationships did not work or why she was disrespected and treated as if she was unworthy. Her new questions were, "What do I need to do God? How can I be a better person?" She expressed to God, in humility, her wrongdoing and desired earnestly to accept his instruction. God heard her cry and acknowledged her sincerity and readiness to move forward with his therapy sessions. Therapy with God was amazing, although not easy. Still, God showed her that she was worth his time and patience.

God taught Sheaba to think in a different way. Rather than thinking about the negative things she had done, she thought about how she could bring those things in subjection to God. As he continued to show her who she was in the flesh, she thought back on her life and all the encounters she had. She recognized the company she kept and her surroundings, which catapulted those behaviors. She could hear the tone of voice she used toward people (mostly men). Her attitude, body language, and choice of words disrespected God's framework. *Wow*, she thought, *only God can cause me to think in that manner.* That thought alone gave her hope that she would be all right.

Sheaba remembered whining to her family and friends about her experiences with men and how she believed they abused and mistreated her. Sheaba being mentally and emotionally messed up for so long, realized that she had never admitted that what some of the men did to her was partially her provoking. She too had a part in prolonging the abuse. In her childhood years, she had screamed *no*, but by the time she was a preteen and older, she never said no; she welcomed it. Why? Because her body had adjusted to the touch of strange people, both men and women.

Although she was full of fear in her young experience and was not to blame, she understood when she had become an adult, that as she began to experience men willingly, she would tell those who desired her intimately "no,", but that really meant yes. Reality is, she thought she was in full control of herself, but was still being controlled by men (her opium addiction). Sheaba felt alone, and was afraid to tell the truth about what she was going through when she was younger because people could not be trusted with her personal pains. It was bound to be held against her in ways that would tarnish her self-image and cause a deeper pain to her soul. She did not want that; the pain was already settled deep in her soul, suicide would have been next. Sheaba thought, *I am sure there are many people with secrets that they are afraid to expose. They may not be as bad as mine, or maybe they are, each one is different but equally painful I bet. It is easy to determine the validity of someone else's issue, but when it is their own, they want it to be handled sensitively. However, I understand that there are always two sides to a story, and there always will be missed information due to the traumatic acts of the situation. Sometimes the one being abused, and have the traumatized mind, can only remember half of the truth, while other areas become blurred or forgotten.*

She continued to reflect on how she justified her wrong doing, and concluded that she had pointed out others' wrongs to cover up her own, which always perpetuated her cry as the victim. It appeared that everyone thought the same way because they were doing the same thing. Sheaba did not understand the procedure to calling out the wrong until she had gone through the therapy sessions with God. People often said to her that she was too old not to understand this or that, when in reality she understood that she was too old, but was truly ignorant to what was wrong. Solely because everything she was doing is what she mirrored growing up. Her surroundings exuded those same behaviors.

Where were those who were supposed to have loved and cared for her? Didn't they know she would live her life outlandishly and uncontrollably after the secret of her childhood was revealed? No, she was deemed the liar, and her molester was the victim of the lie she told. The others lived in the same household and knew what they had done to her, yet when the story of another was revealed, not even they believed her or tried to help.

It was hard to balance being strong in Christ (spirit) and strong in her flesh (humanity). All she wanted was a genuine relationship, but her life was too messed up to attract a man with good sense. Her conversation exposed her way of thinking and always messed up opportunities to be with a man who had his head on straight. Every guy seemed to judge her before and after they introduced to her their opiate drug. Therefore, her defense was always aggression and blackmail, especially if their drug was weak and ineffective. She promised to make them look like fools if they made her look bad by opening their mouths about their business together.

Sheaba had grown to hate men, so she used them to get what she wanted from them and cared less about their feelings. She rarely received tangible things, except a body full of their opiate drug. Though she hated men, she needed them. Without them, her void of loneliness would not be filled, neither would she be relaxed in her pain. Truth is, her pain was not going away; the addiction that lead her to the pushers are what held her bound to her past. In her time of dysfunction, the few men with common sense wanted something real with her, but as she'd been abused, she abused them. When they were too nice, she triggered their bad side so she could test them out, which ran them away. Not understanding, she tried to apologize hoping they would forgive and understand her dysfunction.

Sheaba knew she was dysfunctional in relationships but did not believe it was to her own detriment. She believed being nice, reasonable, thoughtful, and understanding would mask her dysfunction. However, all it took, however, was for a man to disrespect her, and those camouflaged characteristics were exposed and used to tear down every man's ego and break his stride. She was not so innocent after all; she used her past to depict her behaviors as justified. Matthew 7:15 spoke about being aware of false prophets that come in sheep's clothing but are ravening wolves. Although she was not a prophet, she was a wolf that was later exposed. Sheaba's lifestyle proved she needed help, but no one stepped up to help but God.

At each stage of her life, every man she was with fed her dysfunction. The pain was becoming more unbearable and she felt as if life for her was at its wits end. Pressing harder to lean on God's love was her only hope. As she had become a bit grounded in God, ignorant of how to lead her life in Godly relations, she turned men off. In her attempt to explain her relationship with God and how it would benefit their relationship, men viewed it as a negative. They did not understand her walk with God and most had no desire to understand it. Ultimately, things would get worse because their thoughts of God was hogwash. Instead of ending the relationship, she compromised, hoping one day they would meet in the middle. With determination, she tried living and speaking Christ-like among them to help them see the positive in how God changed her, but it only made them angry and more distant.

Each time, the men Sheaba dated lost interest in her and eventually dumped her, or they mistreated her until she got tired of it and left. Sheaba was taught in church that God would choose her man, Sheaba thought, *Where is he? Why was God taking so long?* Later, she found out that God does not choose but approves and allows man and woman to meet on his grounds, through the application of his word from the bible and their prayer life.

Sheaba thought, *That is pretty cool*, but she was very impatient. In her awareness, impatience was recognized as the leading cause of her poor choice in men. Soul tides with them created strongholds that broke her down. Allowing their opiate drugs to enter her body introduced to her every generational curse they encountered. All of her past, and all of their past was being shared equally, which caused wars and fighting between them (James 4:1 NLT), which was why her relationships failed.

To add to the drug addiction (men), Sheaba thought she was good at manipulating men, but she was playing herself. She used her subtle sensuality to attract them. Her response to their calls gave them a sense of belonging, and when they thought they were in control, her attitude and behavior interrupted their manhood. Her tone disrespected their authority, her body language dismembered their hopes of pleasure, and her choice of words destroyed every ounce of good character within them. That secret weapon literally killed the fire in every relationship. When God exposed her behaviors, it backfired on her. In fury, Sheaba intentionally made attempts to tear down the building of man for tearing her down. However, it was not those men who ripped her apart, it was her own actions created by her past. She needed to be remodeled from head to toe and inside out; only God could do that.

In an attempt to get rid of those deep-rooted issues, Sheaba inspired herself to purchase a few books to educate herself on being a lady and positioning herself to be a queen to God first and then to a husband later. The first book she read was *One Night with the King* by Tommy Tenney. Her next study was reading the story of Ruth in the Bible. Desiring to learn more, she watched biblical movies as well about Esther, Ruth and Sarah. Their poise and approach as women were amazing to Sheaba. She had never seen women so feminine and submissive. While studying, her past flashed through her mind, and a pang struck her in the pit of her stomach. As she wondered if she could endure the pain, she understood she could not wallow in it. A more positive thought helped Sheaba to focus on the new life that was about to be born as she changed her life through Christ.

Societal views of those painful memories made her feel as though she asked for what happened in her life. This is not the first time Sheaba felt responsible for her actions; confused at what is her fault and what is not, she felt compelled to reach out to those men of whom she had relations, to ask for forgiveness. Most of her apologies were not accepted, and anxiety gripped her chest hard. Sorrowful for her actions toward them opened her up to vulnerability.

God's presence and her acceptance to him weakened her flesh and strengthened her spirit. However, Sheaba had not tapped into the strength of her spirit as of yet. Therefore, she did not comprehend that God intentions were not to condemn her but to heal her from her past and prevent her from demolishing another man's building. God was not selfishly her builder alone, but everyone's builder. "For every house has a builder; but the one who built everything is God" (Hebrews 3:4 NLT).

Every soul is meaningful to God, and no one person is better than the other. "Be friendly with everyone, don't be proud and feel that you are smarter than others. Make friends with ordinary people" (Romans 12:16 CEV).

He sees the greater good in everyone and desires his love to be evident in all. "Beloved, let us love one another: for love is of God; and everyone that loveth is born of God, and knoweth God" (1 John 4:7 KJV).

Sheaba's therapy sessions with God taught her self-respect. Self-love had not been mastered as of yet, but she felt at peace with the direction progress was leading. Unfortunately, learning to genuinely forgive self and others, her growth sparked her desire, but toward those who showed respect. It is almost as if Sheaba wanted to test each level of growth before God perfected it. Her pusher was obsolete, the desire for opium was gone, but the desire for a healthy relationship was present. Regardless, all she knew were her pushers and that is what she was used too. Men were considered her pushers because she presented herself as an addict. No matter how hard she tried, her body was not strong enough to fight the feeling alone.

Sheaba needed the confusion of her life extinguished, as the destructive paradox only led her back to degradation. The thought of choosing man over God again was debilitating. After all, God was the only one who cared to save her from her drowning experiences. Sheaba was not willing to go down that dark road again. God, in his mercy, did not allow her to damage her faith walk with him; he came through, as always. He rearranged her view of forgiveness through helping her understand, that although forgiveness enhanced love, it did not always restore what had been broken. However, when the right people saw her heart, they embraced it.

> Pardon, I beseech thee, the iniquity of this people according unto the greatness of thy mercy, and as thou hast forgiven this people, from Egypt even until now. And the Lord said, I have pardoned according to thy word; but, as truly as I live, all the earth shall be filled with the glory of the Lord. (Numbers 14:19–22 KJV)

Before God ushered Sheaba into his therapy sessions, she had been suicidal. Although it would not have solved her problems, it certainly would have ended the consistent journey of pain. Ultimately, God was the answer; he had a plan for her life, and the plan was not for her to die:

> For I know the thoughts that I think toward you, saith the Lord, thoughts of peace, and not evil, to give you an expected end. (Jeremiah 29:11–13 KJV)

His plan was for her to die to her flesh and allow his spirit to be made whole, internally, and externally

> I have been crucified with Christ and I no longer live, but Christ lives in me. The life I now live in the body, I live by

faith in the Son of God, who loved me and gave himself
for me. (Galatians 2:20 NIV)

In order to die to her flesh and live, Sheaba was required to give
up everything her flesh desired and trust God to replace them with
his love and life of peace.

Sheba knew that no man, but God, would understand her pain
and tolerate her while she was going through it. No man would be
a comforter when she had flashbacks of various styles of abuse; it
would be used against her. Unfortunately, she believed she would
never experience a healthy romantic relationship. It was important
to understand that man was never created to save her from her past;
only God could do that. Sheaba held on to God for dear life as she
remembered her past. Through all her pondering, God expressed his
jealousy regarding men and other things that she put before him:

For I am jealous for you with a godly jealousy, for I
betrothed you to one husband, so that to Christ I might
present you as a pure virgin. (2 Corinthians 11:2 KJV)

Without fear, Sheaba understood that God would remove
everything in his way if it were served above him. While allowing
every word of each scripture to marinate, she remembered a time
when she experienced God's wrath in a relationship she was pursuing.
God instructed her to end it and declared he would reconcile it at an
appointed time, but she was too attached to let go. She disobeyed his
command, and a year later, the man almost lost his life. God spared
his life, but he knew Sheaba would never leave the man, so God
allowed her to bear the pain and suffering of caring for him for ten
weeks, while another woman was waiting for his recovery. Sheaba
knew about the woman, but she was not aware of the plans the two
had made upon his recovery. When he was released from the hospital,
he married the woman, with no regard for Sheaba's heart. And he
didn't tell Sheaba what he'd done; she found out on social media,
which caused her to have a panic attack.

She was home alone when she discovered the truth. She gasped for air as tears rolled down her face. She looked up and began to pray to God in her mind. Again, God pulled her through it. Questions danced through her mind. *Where was that woman when he needed someone to help him in the hospital? Where was she in the middle of the night when he was confused?* Again, Sheaba learned a valuable lesson and faced another painful reality: never doubt God's voice or commands. Each encounter built a stronger reverence toward God with additional fear.

Sheaba appreciated the flashbacks and reminders of God's love during her therapy sessions. Some brought pain but gave her more wisdom than war. War was only evident when her flesh would attempt to disobey the Spirit of God. Sheaba didn't know what the end result of her therapy would be or how it would preserve her, but she certainly did not trust herself. She believed if she did not stay grounded in God, she would surely go back to the familiar. It was important to trust God, both in and out of his presence. It was the only way she could have permanent change.

> Trust in the Lord with all thine heart and lean not unto thine own understanding, in all thy ways acknowledge him and he shall direct thy paths. (Proverbs 3:5 KJV)

Though Sheaba was getting stronger in her walk with God, it realistically was still quite hard to remain totally optimistic. Sometimes it was hard to apply the scriptures to her life and live by them. Despite all the struggles Sheaba was overcoming, change did not come as fast as she would have liked; God took his time with her. God's rod was always strong when he chastised her, and she understood that it would be that way until she learned to trust him in all things. Getting rid of Sheaba's pushers and the desire to taste the opiate drug, unleashed an anger that was easily triggered. In those times, God immediately dealt with her present experiences:

> Don't be angry or furious. Anger can lead to sin. (Psalms 37:8 CEV)

> A person with a quick temper stirs up arguments and commits a lot of sins. (Proverbs 29:22 CEV)

Basically, anger was not allowed to be her GPS for life. What triggered her anger had the ability to drive her in the wrong direction. By heeding the scriptures, her triggers were subjugated. In her imperfections, making the right decision appeared difficult. Again, God's Word appealed to her situation and told of her weaknesses:

> Therefore, my disquieting thoughts make me respond, even because of my inward agitation. (Job 20:2 NASB)

His Word pressed so deeply into her soul that any thought to do the opposite of what God taught in therapy, would be relinquished. Little by little, different things that were deeply rooted were uprooted. Sheaba did not fight against it, as to do so would mean to remain stagnant—no change and no growth. Messing up meant starting over, and that was not an options. When Sheaba had wayward thoughts, God often disrupted them with chastising scriptures.

> For all this his anger is not turned away, but his hand is stretched out still. (Isaiah 5:25, KJV)

Sheaba did not take God's Word or his therapy sessions for granted. Although she hated his chastising her, she appreciated it. God's chastisement, correction, and reproof (2 Timothy 3:16) did not mean that he had no mercy. He was merciful to her and full of love, the kind of love that surpassed all human understanding (Ephesians 3:19, NIV).

Trusting was tough for Sheaba, but trusting God was essential to her change. Change was not the only goal, but trusting God meant growth in her walk with him and a healthy relationship. God fought for her when no one else would. Regardless of sometimes doubting

God, he never turned away from her and always showed genuine love in his chastening.

One morning during church service, Sheaba realized her indecisive and inconclusive prayers had once again silenced God to her requests. He made it plain that those who come to him must come to him honestly.

> God is a spirit and they that worship him shall worship
> him in spirit and in truth. (John 4:24 KJV)

Sheaba faced God in this area before, so hiding her true desires in her thoughts during prayer was not new. It was evident that God desired to attack those hidden struggles head-on. If she could be real and truthful with herself, she could be real and truthful with God— and by faith, the truth would heal her wounds.

Walking in truth meant living transparent. Allowing God to perform surgery in those deep secret places of your soul. God loved digging deep; his plight was to clean Sheaba out and fill those voids with his Holy Spirit. God, in his omniscience, is aware of all things, told and untold. He always knew what Sheaba was thinking before she thought it (Hebrews 4:12). Therefore, coming clean with how she truthfully felt when praying was in her best interests. Exercising attributes of truth and honesty alone prevented hidden agendas in her closet from embarrassing her later in life; she could be free. Sheaba was grateful to God for his approach, and was thankful for his Word of truth. Now, Sheaba began holding herself accountable for her actions while becoming a true woman of God. Her present focus was being real before God and when in prayer coming before him in truth and in spirit; repenting daily for known and unknown sins.

Sheaba felt like she had graduated to a new level in God and with growth comes new challenges. One of her biggest challenges was temptation, which visited her often. Sometimes she failed, while other times she passed. She thought; *What was the proper way of escape?* She took it to God in prayer and waited to hear his response. Although there was not an immediate response, later, in her private devotion time, a word entered her conscience: "There hath no temptation taken you but such as common to man; but God is faithful, who will not suffer you to be tempted above that ye are able; but will with temptation, also make a way of escape, that ye may be able to bear it" (1 Corinthians 10:13 KJV).

Amazing! Sheaba thought. *God will allow temptation to test my faith, but he won't ever let it control me.* Though at times it seemed overwhelming, God made sure it was bearable—just enough that she would recognize that only God could bring her out of whatever situation she was facing. There was strength in those words, but Sheaba thought, *but what if I did not pass the test? Would she be persecuted by it? Would that be the end of her relationship with God?* God laid this scripture upon her heart:

> Forasmuch then as Christ hath suffered for us in the flesh, arm yourselves likewise with the same mind: for he that hath suffered in the flesh hath ceased from sin; That he no longer should live the rest of his time in the flesh to the lusts of men, but to the will of God. (1 Peter 4:1–2 KJV)

Again amazed, Sheaba thought, *God would literally pick me up where I had fallen and failed him and teach me how to arm herself.* Sheaba did not need to worry about failure; God already knew the weakness of her flesh. As long as she sought him, he knew her flesh would eventually die and give in to his spiritual power. Temptation exemplified a mental slavery; it tricked the mind into doing what felt good to the flesh. Freedom was what Sheaba desired; therefore, it was important to keep the Word of God hidden in her heart to battle against her raging flesh

> I have hidden your word in my heart that I might not sin against you. (Psalms 119:11 NIV)

The more Sheaba grew during her sessions with God, the more she shared her experiences with others. By sharing, she recognized there were others whose hearts were damaged and dysfunctional. People were really messed up by things that happened in their pasts. So, as God taught her, she shared and taught them. Putting God's Word to good use helped her remain grounded. In serving God's people, she bore their burdens—"Bear ye one another's burdens, and so fulfill the law of Christ" (Galatians 6:2 KJV)—which at times caused her pain. She did not believe she was strong enough to handle her issues and others' issues, and she had grown tired of sharing. Although she did not quit, she thought about it. Her testimonies helped others, but they helped her as well; she refused to give up what she started. She went before God, and he said, "If thou faint in the day of adversity, thy strength is small" (Proverbs 24:10 KJV).

Wow, Sheaba thought, *another awakening.* Buckling in the time of storm meant she was not exercising the strength of God but her own. Limited power was not God's option; he wanted more for her. Before she acknowledged God, she had exercised limited power, which allowed people to take advantage of her weaknesses. If she retaliated against them, she showed weakness, but if she walked away, bore the pain, and took it to God, that was considered strength. Even that analogy was amazingly unreal in her carnal mind, but she recognized it as the gift of understanding God's plan for her life. It was true that adversity would come all the days of her life, so she made a choice to hold on to the strength of God. It was her victory!

Sheaba determined that demonic forces would no longer shake her foundation. It was her duty to continue sharing her testimony with people, and whenever weariness or the overwhelming feeling of others issues encompassed her, she would release those emotions to God in prayer and leave it with him. God proved that in her obedience and diligence to serve him, his grace would reign, rest, rule, and abide in her life.

> My grace is sufficient for thee: for my strength is made perfect in weakness. Most gladly therefore will I rather glory in my infirmities that the power of Christ may rest upon me. (2 Corinthians 12:9 KJV)

God had taught Sheaba how to trust him, but she realized there were levels of trusting God. Sheaba learned previously that God would be there for her in all situations and bring her out. His instantaneous results early in her walk with him helped her excel in trusting him but struggled with it during times of storms when they were prolonged. A worrywart she had become, and this is how he encouraged her.

> But the God of all grace, who hath called us unto his eternal glory by Christ Jesus, after that ye have suffered a while, make you perfect, stablish, strengthen, settle you. (1 Peter 5:10 KJV)

She was confused at first, as it seemed that God wanted her to suffer. It certainly was not his desire, but he knew that the world would bring suffering for his name's sake. He explained that if she suffered for his name's sake, then her foundation would be made stronger in him, and peace would abide in the midst of the storms of life.

> I have said these things to you, that in me you may have peace. In the world, you will have tribulation, but take heart; I have overcome the world. (John 16:33 ESV)
>
> And ye shall be hated of all men for my name's sake; but he that endureth to the end shall be saved. (Matthew 10:22 KJV)

When Sheaba surrendered things to God, God taught her of his sufferings and how she would have to endure them through his strength alone. In her sessions with God, self-reflection helped her see the ugly reality of her past and pushed her to a new level—still painful but rewarding. At times she believed that not everything that was revealed was true of her. However, it was important to remind herself of the power of an all-knowing God. Accepting what he revealed about her was challenging, but his truth was definite—*if God said it, it was true*, she thought.

> God is not a man, that he should lie; neither the Son of
> man, that he should repent: hath he said, and shall he not
> do it? Or hath he spoken, and shall he not make it good?
> (Numbers 23:19 KJV)

God loved working with Sheaba because of her ability to learn quickly. Having a desire to be transformed by her king to rid addiction and aggression. Allowing God to open her eyes to new ways of living released her ability to respect life. At first it was tough to believe that almost everything she'd learned since birth—outside of the Bible— was typically a lie. She was fighting the wrong way and for the wrong cause. The built-up hate she had should not have been toward people but toward those evil spirits that dwelled within them, which used them against her and others.

In her carnal mind, Sheaba believed that revenge was warranted, and those who did wrong to her deserved to suffer and/or die. In spiritual reality, God wanted her to forgive those who were a part of her persecution and mistreatment.

> If someone slaps you on one cheek, don't stop that person
> from slapping you on the other cheek. If someone wants
> to take your coat, don't try to keep it. (Luke 6:29 CEV)
>
> Be ye therefore perfect, even as your Father which is in
> heaven is perfect. (Matthew 5:48 KJV)

Living in the ways of the world appeared easier, as she did not have to forgive or love people despite their wrongs. She did not have to accept persecution or mistreatment and could fulfill the lusts of her flesh with no conscience. Learning her life was a lie caused a war within her body, but God ushered her through it. He taught her to give those battles to him, as they were not hers alone to fight

> And all this assembly shall know that the Lord saveth not
> with a sword and a spear; for the battle is the Lord's, and
> he will give you into our hands. (1 Samuel 17:47 KJV)

The enemy wanted to rule over her life, but God showed up to pour life inside of her, killing the enemy's plan.

> The thief cometh not, but for to kill, and to steal, and to destroy, I am come that they might have life, and that they might have it more abundantly. (John 10:10 KJV)

Now Sheaba could breathe new life and love herself, and because of that, she could love others, even in their evilness. Sheaba developed a stronger prayer life that drew her closer to God, allowing a deeper understanding of who she is to him. Her greatest prayer was that he would enhance her wisdom and knowledge to combat the things of her flesh.

> Wisdom is the principal thing; therefore, get wisdom: and with all thy getting get understanding. (Proverbs 4:7 KJV)

It was evident that the spirit and the flesh warred against each other constantly, because every time she tried to do right by the word of God, there was a fight to do it.

> For the flesh lusteth against the Spirit, and the Spirit against the flesh: and these are contrary the one to the other: so that ye cannot do the things that ye would. (Galatians 5:17 KJV)

Before she could question why the flesh was stubborn, God opened her understanding to the works of the flesh: "Adultery, fornication, uncleanness, lasciviousness [lustfulness], idolatry, witchcraft, hatred, variance [conflict], emulations [imitation], wrath, strife, seditions [troublemaking], heresies [atheism], murders, drunkenness, reveling [riots]" (Galatians 5:19–21 KJV).

Sheaba thought, *That is a lifelong study on how to overcome each one, but it is worth learning how they displease God.* On the contrary, the fruits of the spirit were listed in Galatians 5:22–23 as "love, joy, peace, longsuffering, gentleness, goodness, faith, meekness, temperance: against such there is no law." Although there was much to battle in the flesh, the word of God clarified that it did not take much to overcome it with the fruits of God.

CHAPTER 4

A New Level of Relationships

After several years of therapeutic sessions with God, Sheaba's life was no longer the same. She continued to fight her flesh with fear and trembling unto God, making strong efforts not to allow herself to remain status quo. The spiritual cleansing gave her a new attitude, a new walk, a new intellect, a new sight, and a new way of handling life. She became one of God's "daughters of Zion"—a daughter that was taken out of worldly slavery and brought into a lifetime spiritual relationship of freedom with Christ.

Everything was different than before; no longer was she sinking in deep waters; she was able to swim through it without drowning. Her soul was on fire for God as he lifted her burdens, calmed her fears, and brought peace upon her head and her household. It felt like a dream, but it was totally real. Sheaba never thought she would live with a sense of purpose, because of the constant drama that lived inside. To have a relationship with God was the best thing Sheaba ever could have experienced. How could anyone deny him? Being in a relationship with God gave her purpose; it made her feel adequate, and she had a sense of belonging. She felt needed in the kingdom of God. He made her aware of the gifts and the potential he had given to her to exercise as he saw fit. Sheaba's countenance was filled with a Godly glow each day. Everyone who had known Sheaba knew something was different. It was surprising to Sheaba that they all concluded she had been saved because she had not uttered a word about it to anyone. Some were happy for her, but most shied away.

As God continued to pour his love upon her, unfeigned love was revealed. It was better than any natural man could have ever provided. It was that moment that God took her hand in marriage. God's plan was to give her a new emotion that unleashed a spiritual love with peace that surpassed all human understanding (Philippians 4:7 KJV). Sheaba fell in love with an invisible being and attempted to erase any thoughts of being out of his presence. There were moments she felt empty as if God's presence was absent from her body and mind, and it made her crazy. God's absence meant she was locked in the filthiness of her flesh (2 Corinthians 5:8 KJV).

In reality, at times, it was her fault that God was absent from her body because she welcomed sin and refrained from prayer and repentance. In God's comfort and joy, she relaxed too much, not really needing prayer because everything appeared to be good. That happens at times, but when she realized it, she resumed her prayers. It was hard at first because time spent away from doing it added resistance. She despised those dry places! This happened throughout her relationship with God until she figured out how to combat the resistance and becoming overly relaxed. Those dry places were strongholds that were not visible to the natural eye, but they were able to be felt. Only being in constant prayer would combat strongholds; as God had an all-seeing eye (Proverbs 15:3 KJV).

Now that Sheaba was able to recognize the love relationship she and God had, she fought to keep it. Feeling safe and secure was all she ever wanted in life and now she had it. The idea of being married to God was not something she conjured up. Often, when doing business, it was assumed that she was a married woman. Bashfully, she would say, "I am single." It was frustrating sometimes to hear that because she always wanted to be married naturally. Sheaba thought, *how could I get a natural husband if people thought I was already married?* Instead of Sheaba seeing it as a compliment, it secretly hurt her feelings.

One morning, Sheaba thought it to be a good idea to sign her and the children up for the Alabama Police Fitness Association that was open to the public for membership. Sheaba was the last person in line, so when she approached the window to speak with the enrollment specialist, they had engaged in a heartfelt conversation.

"Hi, my name is Mrs. Smith, how may I assist you today? "Good morning Mrs. Smith, I'd like to obtain a membership today, said Sheaba. The seasoned woman behind the glass said, "May I have you and your husband's information? Sheaba was surprised by the request, and she stared, speechless, at the woman. Mrs. Smith asked again. "Ma'am, may I please have you and your husband's information to start the membership." Finally, Sheaba proclaimed, "I apologize Mrs. Smith, I am not married. It is just for my children and I. Sheaba's eyes welled with tears, while her eyebrows bent into a frown. Mrs. Smith said, "Please do not to act so offended at such an innocent request, consider it as an honorable compliment." Surprised at the woman's comment and embarrassed, Sheaba straightened her face and prepared her response. She smiled and said, "thank you Mrs. Smith, those were some powerful words, and it hit me by surprise. My past gave off a different look, but, the fact that you see me in that light is an honor." Mrs. Smith said, "Ma'am do not thank me for the blessings God poured upon you. Your husband will come soon enough. You carry yourself as a married woman and that is a blessing. Stay there and you will not go wrong." Again, as Sheaba walked out of the building, her heart was warm, but her soul was grieved. Sheaba thought, *in the beginning I felt jilted because if I look to be a married woman how would I ever be approached by a man who desired to take my hand in marriage?* Unfortunately, without the proper income, Sheaba was unable to afford the membership. While heading to her car, she drifted into deep thought. Although Sheaba did not quite receive the compliment at first, she was glad that she was not wearing the look of a harlot seeking attention, which was once her past profile.

Later, Sheaba learned in Bible study that it was important to have a marital relationship with God before getting married.

> Let us rejoice and be glad and give him glory! For the
> wedding of the lamb has come, and his bride has made
> herself ready! (Revelation 19:7 NIV)

She did not quite get it, but she assumed it would help with her
lack of commitment. The thought of being married to God was
exciting, but it was hard to believe she could live up to the standards
of being his wife. Sheaba thought, *how could I be a good wife in
this body of flesh to a God in the spirit? There was no way humanly
possible to be faithful and committed.* Sheaba was committed to
almost anything she loved in the natural, but relationships were a
merry-go-round, always meeting up with pain and suffering, lies
and deceit, *who wants to be committed to that*, she thought? Sheaba
chuckled at the thought of being committed in a marriage with God,
but it sparked curiosity. *Was God teaching me commitment to him so
I could learn to be committed in a natural relationship? What was
God up to? she thought.*

Okay, Sheaba thought, *flesh and spirit do not mix*—God had
taught her that in therapy—*so how could marriage work between God
and me?* As she processed how things went in her therapy sessions,
she pondered with whether she had missed pertinent information. The
therapy sessions between her and God had woven a bond between
them. He took her through a purging process, casting out of her
soul those things that were displeasing to him, and deposited his
Word into her empty womb. *That must have been God's proposal*,
she thought. But none of it was clear. Her natural heart had not yet
aligned with her spiritual mind.

There was no doubt that she was in love with him, but she kept
thinking, *he is a spirit*. Her mind did graduate to think on spiritual
things, but her heart still toggled from natural to spiritual; mostly
because she still desired to feel the love of a natural man. Sheaba
cried out to God, *What manner of marriage would this be with you?*
She said "yes" to his will and ways, but she did not understand the
ramifications of the outcome. Her ability to stay in the relationship
was doubted. She thought, *How can I be faithful to God in my*

inadequacy? She questioned her ability to remain committed to God's love because of her lack of understanding of natural and spiritual love. Doubt caused impatience and impatience caused haste; why would God deal with that? In the back of her mind, she wanted a man of flesh, one whose touch she could actually feel. Immediately, Sheaba dismissed that thought to prevent her emotions from connecting with her hormones.

Sheaba, while still in doubt of being committed to God in a marriage, reverted back to the reading books about Ruth and Esther, which kept her in alignment with God's plan; whether it was with him or with a natural man. It was understood that being in relationship with God alone was best for her at this time in her life. To rush into being with a natural man would only cause her to fail, as she was not fully developed into a woman of God. God spoke to her impatience through reading Romans 8:25— "But if we hope for that we see not, then do we with patience wait for it?" (KJV). God then encouraged her in this way: "And let us not be weary in well doing: for in due season we shall reap, if we faint not" (Galatians 6:9 KJV). God always knew what to say to her and when to say it; she loved that about him.

God put Sheaba to the test of committing to hearing from him in the midst of a crowd, just as she did in her secret place. He did this to make sure she is always listening for his instruction regardless of where she is. One year the church she attended went to a conference in Houston, TX. It was the T. D. Jakes "Woman Thou Art Loosed" conference. Excitement flared up within her, knowing that was a major opportunity to learn more about what God had for her life. That excitement turned into disappointment when she ran into an issue. But God later made a way for that issue to be resolved.

Financial barriers visited her during the time the trip was being planned. Fortunately, she had already paid the registration fee, but she struggled with paying for her flight and hotel. She knew it was in God's plan for her to go, so she hoped for a break-through in her finances. Time was of the essence and she was just about to throw in the towel and back out when the treasurer called her. "Hey Sheaba!

I noticed that you had not paid your balance and was wondering if you were still interested in attending the conference?" "Hi, yes, I am still interested in going! I am just facing a bit of a financial setback." "Well, praise God for the blessing you are about to receive. Another member paid for everything and was unable to go. But, asked if I could apply her payments to someone who needed the help." Sheaba tried to keep calm in her response but failed. As tears flowed down her cheeks, she belted out, "Thank you, Jesus!" Finally, she would be in the presence of a wide variety of diverse individuals who loved God, all under the roof of a mighty man of God. "Yes! Thank him Sheaba!" "Wow! I am ever so grateful! Please tell whomever it was that I truly appreciate the gift." "Will do, said the treasurer." Sheaba got off the phone and continued praising God and enjoyed the rest of the day relaxing in the blessing of God.

The day of their arrival to the conference was overwhelming. Sheaba was very tired and a little sick from the plane ride; she had never flown before, nor had she ever been among so many people in one place. The conference ran for three days, each of which had morning workshops, prayer services, and the evening word. The first and the last night of the conference had a great impact on Sheaba. The first night, T. D. Jakes spoke about the life of Hosea and his wife, Gomer. Her heart felt extreme grief at the life of Gomer, which reminded her of her own past. Sheaba remembered struggling with her emotions on a consistent basis, and God would always be there to pull her out of the mess she created for herself. That is what Hosea did for Gomer. Just as Hosea loved Gomer despite her background, so did God love Sheaba in the same way. The moral of the story of Gomer and Hosea was to point out how much God loved Israel. However, the love story was powerful and meaningful to Sheaba's restorative life.

That night Sheaba grasped the understanding of God's love toward his people. Grateful for this knowledge, Sheaba worshipped him where she sat, wailing from the depth of her soul. She tuned everything and everybody out until she was disturbed separately by two strange women that tapped her on the shoulder and handed her money; they told her God ordered them to do it. How fitting, as

Sheaba had gone to the conference with very little spending money. Sheaba thought, *look at God providing again!* Sheaba gratefully took the money and the ladies prayed over her while she wept. Sheaba went back to her hotel room overwhelmed by the presence of God. Her thoughts ventured back to her being married to God and how he provided despite her disobedience, doubt, and other areas of negativity. She rested on those thoughts in hopes to wake up the next day with clarity on how to commit to God without a negative mindset.

On the last night of the conference, a surprise guest appeared: Juanita Bynum. She once had partnered with Bishop Jakes but was absent for quite some time. When she stepped onstage, the crowd went wild! Her response to them was; "take those same hands and give a shout out to the Lord." Her message spoke about how to address an issue when God shows that you were wrong about a situation and when someone gets hurt behind it. She made a powerful come back and her message was duly received. Sheaba had always known that Juanita or T.D. Jakes would make right what was wrong, but others chose one over the other and stopped following the one they determined to be wrong. God did not allow Sheaba's spirit to choose and she found herself defending both parties. Sheaba believed God would convict either Juanita or Bishop, as they both had a strong relationship with God. Juanita's appearance confirmed Sheaba's strong intuition. It also confirmed that her spirit was in sync with God's spirit. As Juanita confessed, Sheaba's spirit was moved greatly. Her praise and worship was greater than any she had ever experienced. Bishop considered the service was like no other. It was meant for Sheaba to be there, as it was her life-changing moment. It was graduation day, the pinnacle of her growth. During the height of her spiritual praise, she believed she missed a word from the Lord. Sheaba had no clue of what it might have been but realized she actually did miss his spoken word when everyone revealed their interaction, and what he had spoken to them. Sheaba thought, *the moment of being in such a high spirited crowd of people was critical to my belief of weather I could hear and be connected to God at the same time. Does this mean I am*

not ready to be in a marital relationship with God or anyone else?
What did I miss? Why didn't I hear?

Everyone who attended the conference returned home with a
testimony of a word from the Lord, and they acted upon it. Sheaba
received the messages that were taught and applied them to her life,
and she thought that was all there was to get. Two Sundays later,
Sheaba realized many people had left the church they all had been
attending. Lacking the understanding of what was happening, anxiety
set in. As time passed, everything was revealed. It was time for her to
accept her growth and go! The church she had been attending was a
steppingstone toward her future somewhere else. Unaware, God had
been planning a ministry in her womb. The conference was new and
too loud for her to listen to God's still small voice; she was enjoying
the ride from the messages brought forth. Exploring a gift of the works
of God through her was not something she understood or expected.
The only thing that was on Sheaba's mind was understanding her
commitment to God in a relationship. She had no clue she had been
already exercising the gifts of God. Voluntarily, she taught Sunday
school, and led a praise team. Sheaba worked wherever she was
needed in the church—that was ministry. Not really knowing what
to do, confused, she believed she was supposed to obediently move
on to join a new ministry.

Although she felt confused, somehow she knew that was the
right move. She believed, if God took her to it, he would bring her
through it. The leaders he brought her under later were those who
had also attended the conference, which made the move a bit easy.
The first day she attended their service, the power of God moved so
strongly that Sheaba's flesh was almost unable to contain it. God's
presence in that place gripped her body powerfully and convicted all
points of her sin. There was a great discomfort, one that tightened
all of the muscles in her body. Silently, Sheaba fell to the floor on
her knees, with her head bowed to the floor. A praise was rising
from deep within, but somehow she could not push it out. It felt like
a tug-of-war. Her body had become fatigued and her mind raced

rapidly. Conviction was choking her as she listened to those around her praising and wailing before God.

Before she could think another thought, a loud scream came from the depths of her belly. It must have raised a concern because almost immediately she felt a touch on her back as she continued to hear the people praying. It seemed as if everyone stopped their personal prayer and began praying over her. The power of God moved so much so that time appeared extended. Sheaba thought she might have passed out because by the time she was ready to get up from the floor, the pastor was teaching. A couple of people helped her up and assisted her to a chair. At the end of service, she barely said a word to anyone. She took the time to ponder with what she had just experienced. Her mind, still in the spirit realm, was not aware that the church was almost empty. Before the church was totally cleared, she believed she had only been cleansed by the renewing of God's spiritual washing internally. Sheaba still not sure of God's direction, went home without a word to anyone.

In a matter of months, the new church she was attending had grown and moved to a new facility. While there, she began her cleaning ministry. At first, she did not consider it a ministry, but God spoke to the first lady of the church, who confirmed it as such. Sheaba thought ministry meant standing at a speaker's podium in a church pulpit, speaking to a crowd of people. In Sheaba's confirmed ministry, God polished her with commitment and consistency. Every Saturday and Sunday after church she helped the first lady clean.

One morning God spoke with Sheaba and told her to relieve the first lady of those duties and take sole responsibility. The first lady accepted Sheaba's offer, and the Pastor handed her a key to the church. He trusted her to do what she was called to do. During her time of cleaning, God would always meet her there and directed her on what to pray. On this particular day, Sheaba went before God differently. Before she completed the vacuuming, she laid prostrate on the floor, in front of the pulpit and began wailing before God. In that moment, God provided Sheaba with diverse visions. Her prayers were seasoning the altar for the leaders and others who came to receive something from God. Amazingly, God allowed her to see the visions he shared with her privately during prayer in the church services. Immediately, she worshipped him and thanked him for confirming that those visions were truly from him and not something she conjured in her mind. That was the beginning of her committed marital walk with God, now they were about to have a baby.

Sheaba took her ministry seriously and made efforts to press her way, even when she did not feel like going. Week after week, God visited her while cleaning; he continued to confirm his visions in the services. Further, he prompted her to make purchases for the church where needed, which was an addition to her ministry. The leaders of the church were thankful, and they blessed her in many ways for committing to the ministry. As the anointing of God filled her belly, it grew bigger and bigger. His nourishing word provided her with the sustenance and strength she needed to be efficient in carrying on. Sheaba felt good to finally be consistent in something meaningful and positive. The fact that it was for the kingdom of God made it even more exciting. It also felt good to feel God's presence so strongly. The new level of her walk with God appealed greatly to her emotions. It felt as if God was naturally there, and she could feel his touch. In his presence, she never felt fear or worry. There were times she felt evil spirits lurking when she was cleaning the church, but she ignored it and focused on God, who eventually warred it away. Though she could physically feel fear in the pit of her stomach, God provided a sense of security because she trusted him, and he hid her.

Sheaba walked around pregnant with God's gift, and others noticed—although she didn't. She was enjoying her marriage with God, making sure she did not allow anything to cause distraction. In her faithfulness, she continued basking in the presence of God, loving his touch, and walking in a new life, with a new vision.

Somewhere along the line of serving him, something shifted within her. *What is happening?* she thought. *Why the shift? How could it be? Did God depart from me?* It all started when Sheaba enquired about starting a singles ministry. It seemed to be ignored and when she had gone to her Pastor for assistance, she felt shoved to the side. For months, testimonies of how much fun the married couples had on their outings kept gracing the pulpit. Sheaba grew weary of hearing their stories and got jealous. She knew of a man from her young adult years, who had a crush on her, but at the time she was too young; he would always pop up at her mother's house from time to time. Almost immediately the young man popped up at Sheaba's mother's house while visiting one evening. It was definitely temptation that walked through that door and Sheaba was ready to dive into it. This was a distraction that was sure to block her spiritual vision. Spiritual warfare rose up in the members of her body. She could hear her conscious crying out; "No, God! No, God! Please! No, God!" she cried. "Not now!" But, her flesh was subtly giving off vibes that were driving his attention.

The young man was a crush she could have refused, but she did not do it. She had always wanted to get near him, as he appeared to be such a gentleman. He was funny but annoying, yet somehow he captured her heart whenever he graced her presence. Not caring about her faithfulness being challenged, she made a valiant effort to become weak to her flesh. The man asked her out for one date, and then another and another. The last date was on a special holiday; they double dated with another couple, which made the date extra special. At the end of the night, he surprisingly proposed to her. He told Sheaba that he had always said to himself, if he had ever gotten the opportunity, he would ask her to marry him. Feeling a false sense of love, because she had known him for so many years, and he was close to her family, so she accepted his proposal without a doubt. That was the biggest mistake of her life, as she had no idea that she would fall into a web of mess that would force a spiritual miscarriage.

There was no doubt that God was a better man, but the constant chatter about the marriage ministry stirred up her natural desires. The man from her youth entered into her presence with grace and spoke eloquently. He swept her off her feet with his style of dress and that awesome cologne. He was tall and masculine, and his face was as bright as the light of day. He was well-groomed and intelligent. The more they were around one another, the more her prayer life changed, as did everything she had committed to before he came.

God tried reaching her before she ruined their relationship and lose their baby. The evening the two were going to the courthouse to get married, Sheaba felt a punch in the pit of her stomach that caused her to open her eyes before she married the guy. Even though she knew she had forced the connection between her and the guy, she went before God in prayer to get his approval. She knew that gut punch was God beckoning her to stop, but she prayed anyway hoping for a different word of approvement. Regrettably, Sheaba had already entered the courthouse and prepared for the ceremony. Even though she saw all the warning signs, she refused to pull away from her natural emotional attachment. Finally, it was time to meet the judge. As she stood in front of the judge to give her vows to the man she chose to be her husband, she felt that punch in her belly again, harder than the first. As Sheaba stood in front of the judge holding hands and gazing into the eyes of the man she was about to call her husband, God showed her ugly future with him.

Sheaba almost fainted when God whispered in her ear, "Don't do it!" Sheaba closed her eyes, exchanged vows, and in the midst miscarried her spiritual baby. As she and her husband walked away from the judge, instead of feeling joy, Sheaba experienced a sense of unhappiness and uncertainty. From that day forward, her joy spiraled down to an all-time low. Her marriage began to fail immediately, both naturally and spiritually. When all hell broke out in her marriage, she refused to pray because she knew what she had done. So, she had no one to turn to; she was too ashamed to look to God.

God was disappointed by the miscarriage. Although Sheaba deserved it, God chose not to chastise her as hard as he had in her therapy sessions. Instead, he started a new purging process—cleansing, washing, and purifying—as he did when she first came to him. In her despair, she found herself slain before him almost daily. But in almost three months into her marriage, she heard nothing from God. Sheaba did not leave the church; it was still her priority, and she even got her husband to come one or two Sunday's. Sheaba hoped he would get slain in the spirit and continue coming, but nothing ever transpired from his attendance. After that, he never stepped foot in church again.

About a year later, he and Sheaba separated and filed for divorce. Sheaba did not want the divorce, as she felt she needed to bear the burden of her decision and work hard at maintaining the marriage. It was too late; things had become beyond bad, and Sheaba went completely out of her mind. Her Christian morals and values were compromised as she allowed those vicious behaviors to take a toll toward her husband. She hated him and wanted nothing more than to have him out of her life. The divorce process made her crazy, enough to where she began seeing a shrink for a year. Those sessions, along with consistent prayer, helped her stabilize her sanity.

Eventually, church had become obsolete in her life, and she wanted nothing to do with church people. It was not their fault, but according to her heart, everyone was responsible for her losing her spiritual and natural husbands. The world had now reconvened in her space, replacing true joy with one that was temporary. It felt good while it lasted, almost three years, before she recommitted her life to God.

Conviction burdened her soul as she thought about how she lied to herself and God. There were many nights of uncontrolled tears and sleepless nights, coupled with fear of where her life would end up. It was hard to discuss what she was feeling with anyone. The church watched her embarrass herself with her husband, so she was sure they would not listen or care to help, and she did not trust anyone else. Her children were going through their own adult woes, and she dared not plant any of her burdens on them. Feeling hopeless, she started smoking cigarettes and drinking hard alcohol again. Each morning, getting out of bed became harder and harder.

While depression made its way to her heart, God dropped a song deep into her soul during her attempt to rest. She could hear it in her thoughts as clear as if it were playing on the radio. She woke up full of emotion, singing it, crying profusely, and feeling the rooted pain.

"Oh Lord, I'm lying in this place, and I don't know where to go. Oh no, no, no, no, no, no, no, no. I'm lying in my tears, and I don't know what to do. Tell me if I'm going to make it, Lord. I really need a word from you. I'm down on my knees, praying for peace. When is the day for my release? Yeah! Jesus, I got to know. Jesus, I got to know. Jesus, I got to know. I got to know, when will my change come?"

She sang it over and over until she was able to write down all the words, and they sank in her soul. That song resonated in her spirit for months, reminding her of the pain she suffered in her life. *How amazing is that?* she thought. God gave her the rights to her own song in her guilty season, which thrust her yet into change again.

Slowly, Sheaba allowed God to nurse her back to life through his relational touch. Scripture, at that point in her life, was not enough. God knew she needed to be touched, so he met her where she was first. Having no more strength to bare the pain she was encountering, she forced herself to look up toward the sky, and a hard scream came from the depths of her soul yet again, "God!" It was a scream of both passion and anger, which lead her into a conversation with him, as if he were standing right there. God knew she would return; it was just a matter of time. He knew Sheaba's heart toward him; he communed with her in her youth when she knew nothing about him, as well as in her darkest points of life. He predestined the steps of her life and waited for her to acknowledge him. God had never divorced Sheaba, she left him, but he re-married her when she called on his name with sincerity. He made provision to take care of her needs while she was lost in her sin. Again, he took his time, but started the process of impregnating her with his Word again and seasoning her under his anointing. There was no way she could not return; she belonged to God. Without him, her life was counted as garbage (Philippians 3:7-8 NLT).

As Sheaba continued wailing in prayer, she could feel her chest getting heavy, and her throat felt like bricks when she swallowed. Her head felt like it was about to explode, but she softly and humbly asked God for forgiveness and asked him to rekindle their relationship in the beauty of his holiness. Again, he had never left her, she left him. She asked for strength to pull through the barriers she created in her life and to speak life into those she spoke death into. She desired her body to be a vessel of honor, serving him with true conviction, and she accepted the brick upon her head for his name's sake, rather than self-infliction. She hurt so bad that she could not cry anymore, but she did not give up the fight to win her first husband back.

Refusing to feel sorry for herself, she stood up against those monsters she had created in her life. The battle between her flesh and God was yet to be won but not by her hand alone. Though God was silent in pursuing her, she knew he would only let her go so far in her sufferings before he stepped into her recovery process. Sheaba did not want another rescue from God, she thought it to be best that he meets her on the road to recovery. Doing her part to walk in the presence of God and trusting he was there would allow her to see the chains of her past and present break, as she made more fruitful and meaningful interactions with God. The battle was on against her flesh, and prayer continued until she got God's attention. Each day as she walked through her home, she prayed into the atmosphere until there was a reconnection between her and God. There was no time for waddling in her sorrows or feeling unworthy for continuously stepping out of God's alignment. The time was now or never to receive him back into her life.

The day God reconnected with her was through a vision. In the vision, she saw herself treading through thick mud. She tried to make her way out of it, but it was difficult. No matter which direction she went, it was almost impossible to get out of the mud. With no other choice, she took steps through it, but it got deeper, and the heaviness and thickness of it gripped her body. Feeling a bit frustrated and scared, she immediately heard the voice of God. His tone was not as soft as it so often had been it was very strong, so much that it felt like her body was vibrating.

He said, "You walk around thinking you can live life without going through something. You create the filth, but you do not want to walk in it. The longer you live life without me, the heavier the

weight will be upon you, and the deeper you will sink in your mess."
He then showed her coming out of the mud, having not one ounce of
filth, and he spoke again, saying softly, "This is life with me." Those
words caused her belly to do flips, her lips to tremble, and her knees
to become weak. Slowly lowering herself to the floor, she wept with
a sorrowful heart. It was that day when she understood that, as long
as she lived, there would be trials and tribulations. She would not be
exempt from them. It would be her duty to stand on the strength and
promises of God and make reasonable decisions to get through them
without blemish.

Moving forward, Sheaba did not accept defeat. She pressed
through circumstances with her head high and her shoulders relaxed.
Her walk changed from being stiffly oppressed to a walk with poise
in Godly victory.

The Storms and the Gift

After Sheaba raised her hands in praise to God and by faith held
on tightly to God's unchanging hand, she hoped God would take her
hand in marriage again. She moved on the idea that it was time to
change from being a counterfeit Christian to living real before God.
One who understood that in her humanity there will be battles she
would have to fight in her flesh and only God can help her win. The
battles of life were not going anywhere; they were there to build
her faith and strength in God. In order to become victorious, it was
essential to face every battle with God courageously and without
fear. Whenever Sheaba raised her hands to Christ in surrender, the
enemy wasted no time in stepping in and attempting to wreak havoc
in her life.

Sheaba was committed to her job at the County for four years,
however, it took a lot of time away from serving God the way she
desired. Changing shifts here and there helped a little bit, but not
enough to put in the time she needed to strengthen her faith walk
with God. It was fitting to find another job that suited her desired

lifestyle with God. Successfully, she found one that did not take too much of her time. Unfortunately, after ninety days she was relieved of her duties there and struggled to find employment thereafter. Again, she felt helpless and defeated, but reminded herself who she served.

Three months after losing her job, she lost her car insurance and afterwards was rear-ended. The woman at fault in the accident wrote Sheaba a five-hundred–dollar check to cover repairs, but Sheaba refused to accept it because not much damage was done to her vehicle. Besides, the woman was shaken up pretty bad and by her conversation it seemed as if she was financially strained. The woman was persistent; she preferred paying right at the scene of the accident. Sheaba accepted the check and applied it to her past due rent. Sheaba was stressed out with everything that was happening; it was like a domino effect. The money she received from the woman was not enough to cover her bills, so she was forced to withdraw her entire 401(k) investment. Sheaba felt sour in her stomach, as she knew her home would be the next thing she would lose because her investment money did not stretch far enough. The landlords were truly godly in their generosity; they did all they could to help, but they had a mortgage to pay. They allowed her to stay in the home for two weeks without asking for payment. Before Sheaba moved in with a close friend, she left the house spotless and in perfect condition. The friend that Sheaba moved in with would never be forgotten. It felt like Sheaba was in her own home. Her thoughtfulness kept Sheaba from being homeless and for that, she promised to always do whatever she could for her friend without hesitation. Grateful that God provided in such a stressful time, every night before she went to bed and after her friend went to work during the day, Sheaba prayed earnestly.

One Saturday evening, Sheaba was invited to a family member's birthday party at a local bar. One of her ex-boyfriends— who had broken her heart—worked there part-time. When she arrived, her family members were surprised to see her, as she hadn't visited them in over a year. They offered her many alcoholic drinks, but she chose to drink cranberry or orange juice. She turned down many offers to dance and never entered the dance floor to participate in line dancing something she absolutely loved. She did not want to be there because she was not happy with the shift that had recently happened in her life; not to mention the type of crowd there was distasteful. but, she still had fun mingling with family.

Sheaba made her way to the DJ booth to speak to her ex-boyfriend out of respect. It did not take long because there was not much for them to talk about. As she headed back to the bar where her family sat, she suddenly felt uncomfortable and was ready to leave, but she stayed to prevent questions. Her family noticed she was not the same party girl as she was in the past and respected it. As Sheaba sat at the bar watching everyone have a good time, her eyes were locked on the tallest guy in the club. Sheaba thought, *Where did he come from?* She tried hard not to stare at him so she began looking instead looked at her phone, where she saw a notification for an unread text message. She was reluctant to open it because it was from her ex. Instead of opening the text, she gazed over at the dj booth where she noticed he was waving to her to come over. The tall guy was standing next to him and that made her nervous. Oddly, she wanted to get to know him, hoping she could flirt with him. She walked over to her ex keeping her eyes off the tall guy. Sheaba wondered if the woman he was dancing with earlier in the night was his wife; she had hoped not. When she had finally approached her ex, he asked Sheaba, "Do you remember Jack?" Feeling insulted, she looked at her ex with a scowl; she thought he saw her staring at him and was about to create an issue out of it. He recognized the look in her eyes and said, "I introduced him to you while back." Sheaba said, "No, I do not remember Jack. Is that all you wanted?" Before she could answer, she turned around, shook Jack's hand, spoke, and attempted to walk away. Jack called out to her, "Hey! You know my cousin Lucy?" That caught her attention. She cuffed her mouth in astonishment! "You are Bernita's son? Jack said, "yes!" Lucy had talked about Jack from time to time, but she had no idea Jack was the son of Bernita. Bernita was Sheaba's spiritual mother, which is how she met Lucy.

Sheaba hugged Jack and said, "it was great to finally meet you." They must have talked too long because the lady he was with got kind of antsy. Out of respect, she ended the conversation and said, "I apologize, I had no idea you were with a woman. Will you please properly introduce us? I don't want any trouble." Quickly he stated, "I am not married, I am single. She is not my woman; she will be alright." Sheaba walked away immediately because she could tell the woman was furious. Sheaba, not paying any attention to Jack or the woman again, did not realize the woman was walking around the bar watching her. Sheaba figured it was best to leave, but as she was about to walk toward the door, she noticed the woman sitting at a table in front of her. She caught the woman looking up at her with a scowl on her face as if she wanted to fight. Sheaba, not wanting any trouble, touched the lady on her shoulder and got eye level with her and said, "ma'am I do apologize, my name is Sheaba, I meant no harm. I know Jack's mother and cousin and got caught up in conversation, I didn't know he was with you." The woman frowned even harder and said, "take your hands off of me and don't say another word to me. You don't know me." Sheaba backed off and prepared to leave, but Jack called her over again. She hesitated and then walked to him. He asked, "may I have your cell number? I have some things I'd like to ask you." Sheaba did not know how to respond to that after the woman had been so mean. "Why? Sheaba asked. Jack said, "I will discuss that with you later if you don't mind." Sheaba looked around to see if the woman had come closer, as she truly did not want any trouble. Sheaba said to Jack, "your friend is following me around the bar looking at me like she wants to start something. It would be fitting for you to talk with her, as I will not be fighting anyone, especially in a bar." Jack said, "Just ignore her, she is drunk and acting out. Sheaba said, "That is kind of hard to do seeing how she is behaving, I have to make sure she doesn't actually attack me." As Sheaba headed for the door and to her car, she made sure she was not being followed by the lady.

The next evening, Jack called and properly introduced himself. "Good morning Sheaba this is Jack, we met at the bar last night. "Good Morning Jack! How are you this morning," said Sheaba? Out of curiosity Sheaba said, "what is the reason for this call? What is pressing that you needed to get my number and call me? I truly do not want to deal with your lady friend and her nasty attitude. Does she live with you?" "Yes," he said. "Please don't worry about that. I just thought I heard you mention a name of someone I had a past with last night and was curious as to how you know them." Sheaba explained, "I am not sure whom you are speaking of, however, Lucy and I met through your mother and she never expressed anything of your personal business. It is your mother and I that are close." As for your mother, she is not big on sharing anything personal about herself or anyone else" "Your mother has been an encouragement to me for a couple years." "I had no idea you were her son. She briefly spoke of you, but again, I had no clue it was you because she never mentioned your name, she would always address you in conversation as her son. I am not sure what you heard, but it is no reason to be alarmed." Jack said, "that is cool. Sometimes my family could talk too much about other people's business." Sheaba said, "Well your secrets are safe, whatever they are." Jack responded, "There are no secrets, but my personal information should be shared by no one but me." Sheaba responded, "absolutely. Now is there anything else I can help you with?" Jack said, "No. But we will talk again, right?" "Maybe, said Sheaba. The call ended and Sheaba felt relieved, as she certainly felt awkward with the questions he asked. It was odd that he believed his family would tell a stranger his business. His cousin and his mother had never behaved that way in her presence.

The phone calls continued between the two for about a month. By then, he had assured her that the woman was out of his presence and not aware of their phone conversations. Each time they talked for hours, mostly about her past relationship with her ex, who happened to be Jack's childhood friend, and was still friends. She allowed that conversation for no more than a month, and then she cut it short, as it was not good rehashing old wounds, especially after God brought her through them.

Jack called often until they started bumping heads, and they would go without calling each other for months. Talking to Jack about her ex brought out a lot of anger, which made Sheaba wonder if she was freed from those past hurts or still holding on to some of them.

Despite all that Sheaba had been going through and all that she had lost, her walk with God was still going strong. Love was real again between Sheaba and God. She resumed her cleaning ministry at church, and later excelled to new levels of ministry. Without being asked, Sheaba made a point to make sure the first lady of the church was not overwhelmed with handling many projects alone. The church was small, but there was so many things that needed to be done. Sheaba loved serving the church because her mind felt free of the negative thoughts that often lead her to troublesome behaviors.

During one morning service, God challenged Sheaba at prayer time.to do something she had never done before. In the midst of prayer God showed Sheaba in a vision crawling to the first lady of the church feet. At first, Sheaba was hesitant, but she knew obedience was better than sacrifice. Not wanting to make a fool of herself, she continued in prayer and didn't move. But God continued with the vision, so Sheaba trusted him and moved. She crawled from where she was seated to the feet of the first lady, who stood at the alter praying for another. Sheaba gently grabbed the first ladies ankles and laid her face on her feet and prayed. Not knowing exactly what God wanted her to pray, she wailed and then quietly whimpered to listening for instructions. Suddenly she felt a touch on her back, God spoke to her conscious. Sheaba entered into a new level of ministry; she was to sit at the feet of the first lady of the church service her and be fed wisdom under her leadership. The first lady laid praying hands on Sheaba before she raised up from her feet; humbly she laid there until she was finish. A spoken word through the first lady was "put on the robe of Christ and never take it off, God has clothed you with it."

Wow, Sheaba thought, *what does that mean?* God first gave instructions and then a blessing, and she rested in that. As she attempted to raise herself from the floor, her knees buckled. First lady caught her under her arms and leaned her into her bosom and whispered, "God no longer wants you on the floor, he has strengthened you to stand in your weakness." At the end of Church service, Sheaba chuckled at her experience during service. She told of how embarrassed she was at the thought of carrying out what God had given her the vision to do. Happy that she did it, hugged every individual who surrounded her and expressed her love and gratitude for their love and support.

Since that time, the first lady and Sheaba had grown extremely close. Sheaba tiptoed around her a little bit because she still had to learn how to walk in the ministry of being at her feet. She was always afraid of doing or saying the wrong thing. As they learned more about one another, God imposed a trustworthy bond, as well as a connection where Sheaba understood what she needed before asked. Sheaba took initiative and learned how to effectively service the first lady with trial and error. Although there were some emotional moments, Sheaba's ministry had grown solid in her approach and commitment. Everything moved smoothly and as God planned.

In Sheaba's growth, she held herself accountable to the tasks she was given. Peace amazingly sat on her like two doves on a branch; in that, humility clothed her, and faith fashioned her. Sheaba felt like a little child as she served under the leadership of the first lady of the church; but it was where God wanted her at that time in ministry. Both the pastor and his wife were always there for her in the time of distress; teaching her how to recognize when to battle and when to allow God to battle on her behalf.

After a while, God limited their availability, to teach her how to lean on him and not humanity. When she faced those low moments of her life, she needed to know how to go to God first. Sheaba understood that with growth in God, there will always be attacks from the enemy. Two months had gone by and she had not heard from Jack, so she assumed he and his lady was doing better. She supposed it was best they were not in contact because he always found a way to rub her the wrong way. It was kind of attractive though; he challenged her to think deeper in the natural realm. All Sheaba knew was spirituality and had not learned how to balance the spiritual and the natural when she would fall into diverse temptations. Reverting to the natural during a time of temptation was more comfortable and familiar than the spiritual.

It was almost as if Jack heard her thoughts because one week later, Jack called. Nervously, she answered the call; wondering what his conversation would be since their last hang-up. At first, she thought he would ask why she hadn't called; but he just rambled on about things like books, religion, children, vacations, and a bit of venting about relationships. They stayed away from making any comments about being attracted to one another. Sheaba wanted to say something but was not sure if he felt what she was feeling. Sheaba didn't know why she was attracted to him; he would always annoy her in ways that made her not want to talk to him anymore. They had been talking on the phone for about a year, missing a few months here and there, and they developed a good friendship.

Despite Sheaba's attraction to Jack, she honestly had no intention of dating him; again, he was interestingly annoying and was her ex's childhood friend. Besides, he lived in a different city, and there too many things that did not sit well in her spirit about him. Technically, it was dangerous for her to be interacting with any man because she was not good at controlling her emotions. She reminded herself of a previous situation with a man, where she divorced God and lost their spiritual baby. She was certain she did not want to repeat that cycle. However, the more she talked to Jack the deeper the attraction. Disappointed in herself, she thought, *Here I go again, trusting another man. Jack appeared to be loving and concerned, but maybe he was just fishing for information.*

She was disgusted that she always over socialized, and she hoped that it was not too late to pull away from him. Again, she started ignoring his calls for a about a month. He did not call a lot, but when he did, she was reluctant to answer it. Although Sheaba was raised among boys, she had never learned their apprehensive side. Relating to the physical part of man was all she knew; and men were powerful once they were in control. It was hard to distinguish whether they were real or fake when they showed their sensitive sides. Because she was sensitive, she was drawn to their sensitivity.

Standing firm on not talking to Jack worked out well, as he was not a pushy person; he too backed off. In a long stretch of time apart, Sheaba would at times feel an attraction that superseded her odd feelings toward Jack. She ignored the taste for her coitus drug when it revisited. Sheaba knew it was not a test from God because he would not tempt her. However, the enemy of her flesh would definitely unleash that kind of temptation. Instead of worrying about the temptation revisiting her, she tried channeling those thoughts toward the Lord. Keeping her relationship strong and intact with God was important to Sheaba, but it was always a struggle to maintain in her humanity.

Was It to Be or Not to Be?

Sheaba had been nearly free of her desperate desire to be in the arms of a man, however her proclivity toward self-gratification had become an issue in her mentally vulnerable moments. The unimaginable inclination of her flesh was a stronghold that was either satisfied or suppressed. At times, reading the Word of God alleviated those flare-ups at their inception, but even still it was not easy to move through those flames that burned so deep within. It took a long time to find scriptures to battle that beast within, but she did not give up. She understood that self-gratification would move her to angry places in her life, which made her feel grimy and disconnected from her spiritual side.

She choose to read two of her favorite scriptures that were swords to her weakness:

> For though we walk in the flesh, we do not war after the flesh, for the weapons of our warfare are not carnal, but mighty through God, to the pulling down of strongholds, casting down imaginations, and every high thing that exalteth itself against the knowledge of God; bringing into captivity every thought to the obedience of Christ. (2 Corinthians 10:4–6 KJV)

> Finally, brethren, whatsoever things are true, whatsoever
> things are honest, whatsoever things are just, whatsoever
> things are pure, whatsoever things are lovely, whatsoever
> things are of good report, if there be any virtue, if there be
> any praise, think on these things. (Philippians 4:9)

When she could not fight, she would put on her spiritual armor and let it take its course. It always made her chuckle how her mind was so easily influenced by the Word of God. The struggle had been real in time past, but presently, the only struggle was fighting against self. The fight was real! Any time Sheaba moved to a new level in God, the attack of the enemy came that much harder. She chuckled that he watched her the way people watched TV.

Although she had taken time off from talking to Jack, she started to miss him. Eventually, she called him, and they picked up where they had left off. Neither of them remembered what the other looked like since the last time they had seen each other, so they sent their most recent pictures via cell phone. Somehow, Sheaba knew it was a mistake to call him, as she did it out of fleshly emotion. Not one time did she go before God to cover herself from the enemy's plight. Jack had stolen Sheaba's heart a long time ago, but she ignored it. Whenever she thought of him, butterflies turned in her stomach. It was not often, but when it happened, she would feel a sense of joy.

Sheaba fought as hard as she could each time to build her muscles against the feelings, she gained for Jack—. Jack finally expressed how much he missed her and how he is strongly attracted to her. Nervously Sheaba expressed her attraction as well. Unfortunately, as soon as she expressed she thought about how daunting it was that Jack could trigger her indignation. It was a clear indication that they were not destined to be a couple; they would be in constant battle. Jack spoke eloquently and appeared genuine in his approach. He chose his words carefully, which was attractive but a bit frightening. After all, he did say his profession was counseling.

Jack asked, "Sheaba are you feeling anything odd between us?" "What do you mean, said Sheaba. "Personally, I look forward to hearing from you and when I don't I miss you." "whoa! I guess I did not want to acknowledge that same feeling. But it has been that way for me for quite some time now. However, I prefer to leave it as just an acknowledgement." Jack responded sheepishly, "it's cool. I just wanted to know. After expressing their feelings, Jack volunteered to give his opinion of Sheaba. "Sheaba I could tell right away you were a bitter and disgruntled woman who had been through more than you have shared with me. I can help you through it if you let me." Sheaba held on to silence for dear life; she did not want to come off as the woman he had just described. "Hello! Are you still there?" Calmly, she acknowledged him. "Yes! I am just a bit shocked you felt so comfortable to say such a negative thing about me." Her response was respectful but firm, as she did not take kindly to his observation. Their conversation was an extended one that took up the majority of her day. Sheaba asked many questions to get to the bottom of why he had analyzed her the way he had, as well as grilling him to find out more about his life and past history. He shared truthfully as far as she could tell. He was right about most of what he said about her, and it moved her to tears. At that point she was done talking with him. They always ended up in a debate that ultimately resulted in having no contact for a while. Although Sheaba admitted her annoyance with him, he acted as if nothing she said bothered him.

After that last conversation, Sheaba and Jack, again, did not speak for a couple months. Sheaba's attraction had grown stronger; she still experienced those butterfly moments when she thought of him and smiled. It was odd, but it always seemed as if she would get those feelings more on a Sunday; it was on that day that she shared with her children about her sporadic feelings toward Jack. Sheaba did not understand why she was attracted to a man who angered her as often as he did; but at times hoped that someone would help her with reasons not date him; however, no one did. Everyone she told was cheering her on, hoping for happiness. Her children told her to be careful because he was a friend of an ex-boyfriend. Her happiness meant everything to her children, but they did not discount her feelings for Jack. They just wanted her to be sure of whatever decision she made.

Finally, Jack called. "Hello Sheaba. "I will be in your area on a business trip, and would like to take you to lunch if you are not busy." "Yes, I have some things to take care of, but let me know when you get in town and we will go from there." "Great! I will call you when I get in town." Sheaba's mind said turn him down, but her heart said no. She was actually looking forward to seeing him. It had been almost two years since they had seen each other face-to-face. Sheaba immediately felt stressed and pressed for time because she had a lot to do that day. She had just completed her last task when Jack called to inform that he was done with his business and ready to meet. Jack did not hesitate calling her He called multiple times to check on how close she was to meeting him and to remind her how interested he was in seeing her.

As she drove to the meeting place, she prepared her mind and heart to be attached to the Word of God, as she did not want to seem to be desperately seeking for a man. Jack had already had his perception of her personality and so she had to show him self-control. She also made herself look less attractive than usual, as she did not want him to look at her as a product. As she neared her destination, she called him to get his exact location and a description of his clothes. They met near a cookie shop at a local downtown mall where they greeted each other with a smile and a hug. They ventured to the food court and enjoyed a small deli meal and then shared some ice cream for dessert.

Jack suggested they take a ride along the lake before he headed back home. He had traveled by train, so Sheaba allowed him to drive her car to escort her there. When they arrived, they got out of the car and walked for a little while, but Sheaba's fear of bugs forced them to return to the car. The entire time he held her hand, and when they reached the car, he opened her door for her and shut it. While embracing that moment, emotions of a strong attraction raged inside of her. Her heart was pounding with excitement. He was gorgeous, his cologne was breathtaking, and his hands totally covered hers. The feeling was so amazing she almost started crying.

Immediately she began to talk to herself. *Calm down, Sheaba. This is a friend, not a prospect!* She could not look at him when they were talking because she had thoughts of kissing him. His lips were full, and his mustache was lined perfectly above them. She hoped he didn't notice her nervousness when she glanced at him every so often., to let him know she was paying attention.

Time had expired for him; he had to return to his hometown. As they drove to the train station, there was silence. Once they arrived, they exited the vehicle and embraced, this time longer than the first. While her face was buried in his chest, she closed her eyes and wished she did not have to let go. Before Jack walked away, he held the driver door of the vehicle open for her to enter and closed the door. Sheaba raised the window down, waved and smiled at him.

Watching him walk away hurt her; it was as if she was allowing her soul mate to escape. Tears formed in Sheaba's eyes at the thought of having that feeling for eternity. What was comforting is she shared those same feelings for God. It was Sheaba's dream to have a man that made her feel heavenly inside; and that is what she felt at that moment with Jack. It was rather alarming that this man, who was nothing more than a friend, could pull that out of her. *What's happening?* she thought. *Am I that desperate for love, or is God finally allowing me to have relationship with a man of flesh? Is this the one?*

Immediately, when she arrived home, she sought God regarding her encounter with Jack. She refused to fall back into a pit of pain, so she made an effort to get God's consent on her situation. Her heart was feeling him something crazy, and the thoughts of his annoying behaviors were forgotten. As she patiently waited for God to respond, she continued having conversations with Jack. It did not take much for her to fall in love, and she despised that about herself. Although Jack seemed to be a different breed of man, she should have had better control of her emotions. Continuing to give God the same time as she did before she met Jack was already compromised, but she fought to hold on to what she had left in her toward him. Jack was becoming an idol that Sheaba worshipped. It was clear, but Sheaba closed her eyes and kept moving forward.

Sheaba did not know where to begin. Reaching back to her Therapeutic sessions, she tried recapping God's teaching of true love. When Jack would call, his voice accentuated the sound of true love. Jacks calls flowed daily and sometimes more than once a day. Sheaba had been swept off of her feet and had a greater desire to see him more often. She often felt his love energy through the phone without him ever mentioning his love for her. Sheaba gave up trying to refrain from the deep emotions that had heightened for Jack and rested completely in it. Jack was a natural. He knew what to say to Sheaba to get her going emotionally. On one of their phone conversations he declared, "I am not the kind of man to pursue women, they normally chose me." Sheaba was not sure why he made that statement, he had already chose her she thought.

Jack finally revealed that his feelings were changing toward her beyond friendship. He said, "Sheaba I have feelings beyond what we have now and so I would like to pay for your train ticket to visit me for a weekend to discuss where we go from here. Excited about the suggestion, Sheaba immediately agreed. As the weekend was approaching, she realized that she had not consulted God about it, and attempted to recant her agreement.

Sheaba asked herself, *What are you doing?* As she cried out to God, she felt convicted for accepting an offer without consulting him first. She lay prostrate on the floor in silence, listening for God's commands; he was silent. She was afraid that she had gone too far and had disobeyed God. She made the decision to call Jack to let him know she had changed her mind. Of course, he was disappointed; he even sounded a bit upset. *Uh Oh!* she thought. *Maybe Jack will give her a reason to reject the visit by showing his true colors. Surely there is another side to all that macho man. Maybe he was playing me to see how far he could get, and then dump me. Nobody had ever showed love to her the way he did, so she was attached by that alone.*

After expressing her reasons for canceling the trip, a day later, there was no call from jack, so she assumed he was not happy, and she was fine with that. However, the next day, he called, but she did not answer. That evening, she returned his call. At this point Jack was stating his case as to why she should come. "Sheaba, I am not sure why you are uncomfortable coming, but I want you to know that everything will be ok." Sheaba said, "I have changed my mind, I will be there. You are right, I do need a vacation." Instead of Jack being ok with that, he began to say, "What changed your mind? Please do not feel obligated; I just thought it would be a good idea since you had been through so much." Sheaba sat quietly as she processed what had just occurred. "Are you still there?" Jack asked. "Yes, I am here. If you would like for me to still visit you, I am there, if not, that is fine as well." Jack replied, "Of course I want you to come. I do not see why you turned it down in the first place. Anyway, I have your ticket available, so please take advantage of it. The downside of this is, I had taken off work to spend time with you and when you decided not to come I picked up the hours. However, I will see if I can get someone to come in for me." "I apologize Jack! I did not intend to make this such a big issue." Thank you for the invite." said Sheaba. "Great, call me when you get off the train and I will pick you up." "Ok, I will do that." She felt guilty and ashamed that she had moved out of alignment with God and made the decision to visit Jack. Unfortunately, she set herself up for a let-down. When Sheaba arrived at the train station, Jack was already outside of the station waiting for her. When she called, he directed her to walk to where he was parked waiting. As she neared his destination, he met her and grabbed her luggage. They embraced, he put her luggage in the cab portion of his truck opened the passenger door of the truck and helped her inside. He talked to her the entire way to his house, and Sheaba listened while daydreaming of how their time together might be. Gratefully, Jack showed her an awesome time, so much so that he asked her to stay an extra day.

Later, she wished she had not stayed the extra day because they allowed their innocent weekend to be compromised. He touched her in a tickle spot, which was her lower abdomen area. Rather than laughing, she controlled it and her body jumped. Jack's reaction was unbelievable and caught Sheaba off guard. That night was a nightmare; she would never forget the sound of anger in Jack's voice—. She felt violated by his tone and disrespected by his behavior toward her. Sheaba did not understand his gripe. He eventually told Sheaba that he had a problem with her not looking at him when he was making an effort to apologize for misunderstanding her body language. He said it was important for his woman to look at him so that he know she is sincerely receiving what he was saying to her. Sheaba had her back turned to him when he was talking to her, but she had no idea that his attitude would be so strongly exerted because of that. Surprised at his explanation, Sheaba laid silently not knowing what to say. At this point she did not like his demonstrative behavior toward her and was ready to go home. Stubbornly, Jack made it plain that he did not desire to be near Sheaba. He got out of bed and sat in the chair next to it. After trying several times to calm Jack, she decided to leave him alone and go to sleep. She was drained by the event that had taken place. When she woke up the next morning, Jack was lying next to her. The sun was shining brightly in the room, which forced her to think of God. She thanked God for getting her through that horrific night and allowing her the opportunity to see another day, and to hopefully make better decisions.

While waiting for him to awake, her mind replayed the scenario of the previous night in detail, as she tried to figure out what caused the demon to show his face. Feeling ashamed, she declared in her heart that no matter what, she would cut him out of her life and never look back. It took everything in her not to act out of character, as she was disgusted with how he had treated her While her mind was running, he had awakened and grabbed her hand. They lay that way in silence for quite some time before he spoke. He explained the situation in greater detail and why it caused him to be in a rage the previous night and apologized profusely. Although Sheaba accepted his apology, she was in a hurry to get away from him. It was not enough to tell her heart that he would never act like that towards her again. The ride to the train station was quiet. When they arrived, he kissed her on the lips and hugged her, but it did not feel the same as the first time. As she turned to walk away, discomfort filled her joints, but she never looked back.

Three months passed before she heard from Jack, so before he called, she believed they were on the same page of never having contact again. One afternoon Sheaba was heading to the gym when she noticed a missed call on her phone. The call was from him. She did miss him a little bit, but she could not deal with the anger she experienced. That evening, before she went to bed, he called again; she refused to pick up. The next morning, he called, and she watched it ring while talking to herself: *I'm not going to answer the phone and get caught up in his macho charade.* He waited an hour, and then called again, but she still did not answer.

He finally sent a text and expressed how much he missed her. He said he believed he had fallen in love with her. He said he had not stopped thinking about her since she left. Sheaba tried very hard not to respond, but she broke down and responded anyway. They talked that night and settled a few things regarding their quirks, likes and dislikes. Jack said, *"Sheaba, I know we got off on the wrong foot; I know that our last moment together may have not settled in your heart, but if you forgive me and trust me, I will show you I am not that man you seen. I don't want to live another day without you being here with me."* Sheaba sat silent for a moment pondering with what was said. Jack waited patiently for her response. *"Yes, said Sheaba, I would love to be there with you, however, I must pray for guidance, make preparations to transfer my job, and find a place to stay." "For certain, I will not live in sin. I already made the mistake of having relations with you on one occasion which caused our displacement."* Jack said, *"I have an empty apartment across the hall from my apartment that you could take if you like. If you cannot transfer your job and have to find another, you are welcome to stay rent free until you get on your feet."*

That was a great idea, Sheaba thought. *"Thank you, if it comes to that, I will take you up on that offer."*

Sheaba was unable to transfer her job, however, within a month she was called for an interview for an Administrative position in the suburbs of where he lived and was hired on the spot. One week later, she found herself moving in with Jack, as the apartment he'd offered to her was not in a unfavorable condition. Sheaba knew it was a bad idea to stay in Jack's apartment, but she had already moved her things. Sheaba did not tell her family and friends about her move until the last minute. She thought it was best so they had no time to talk her out of it. After telling them, her children were excited, but everyone else was skeptical of the relationship. They knew nothing about Jack. Although Sheaba was excited, she was afraid of what the outcome would be, especially since they were living together out of wedlock.

He was all over her in that first month together. It was sort of scary, as no one had ever shown such interest and love toward her. She was a bit reserved and reluctant to return the same feelings, but she watched and listened to Jack every day. One morning she woke up to find flowers but Jack was not home; it was weird because he had never left her at the house alone. Sheaba thought he had cameras in the house because as soon as she got up and saw the flowers, he called. He said he was at the beach, sitting and thinking about a lot.

She found his next words overwhelmingly odd—he said that he couldn't stop thinking of her and how she made him feel, and he asked her to marry him. He suggested they get married two weeks from that day. Sheaba was speechless, and she wondered if it was a bad idea. She made a promise to herself that she would never again marry in the courthouse; but she accepted his offer.

Prior to that day, Sheaba had freaked out about living in a house with a man when they weren't married, not to mention the experience she had with Jack on her first visit. None of what was happening seemed real. Her heartbeat at sixty miles per hour whenever she thought of her position. Although she desired to have a husband, she knew doing it on a whim was a sign of a bad outcome. Sheaba had fallen in love with the idea of being single. Her time with God was precious; without it, she was lost, and her day seemed off. Being in the arms of a man was not something she planned, especially not that soon. Although it had been six years since her first marriage had ended, she was not sure if she was ready, but was willing to try it again. Sheaba thought, *Heck I am a grown woman, well into womanhood, I am living in my daughter's home, struggling to find my own home with the small amount of money I make, why not give it a try to see where it goes.*

Sheaba always prayed too late, especially when it was about a man. It was no reason to go before God if her mind was already made up, but she did it anyway. Prayer had gone forth previously, but God had been silent, and she assumed God had already approved her relationship with Jack. Everything Jack did was great, except for the one incident, so why shouldn't he be given a shot at marriage with her. While in prayer, her mind raced with doubt. Sheaba knew what to do, marrying him was not the answer at that moment, however, she chose to irresponsibly indulge. Jack was a rare kind and had always been on her mind. He warmed her heart in the most beautiful way. He did not make her feel like he was hunting for meat but treated her like a princess who had no flaws.

Sheaba and the first lady of the church she attended bond was tight. The commitment she made to her and the church was about to be compromised. That alone hurt Sheaba because their relationship was more than a natural one, but a ministry. All Sheaba wanted was to be happy in an all-around fulfilled relationship for once in her life. She wanted the approval of everyone, but that did not happen. Although Sheaba's first lady and best friend gave their blessings, she knew they were just accepting her decision, but wanted to decline her decision. They loved her too much to break her heart, however, they knew it was a big mistake. Her sudden decision to depart from ministry and leave the state was painful to some and sad to others. The fact that no one had the opportunity to meet Jack, caused a bit of concern, at least for her spiritual leaders. Sheaba felt bad, but did not want to change her mind about her decision, so she ignored the disappointments and excitedly moved forward.

On their wedding day, they were full of joy and excitement; it was a day like no other. It certainly was different from her first marriage. They stood before the judge in the courthouse, staring at one another in amazement and with deep feelings of love. The wedding was over within five minutes. They walked out of the courthouse without any thoughts of the previous days but only what they were experiencing that moment.

It was a bitterly cold day, but the sun was shining brightly and the birds were soaring freely in the air, chirping happily. They looked at each other and smiled really big. The remainder of the day was outstanding, filled with music, dancing, and their choice of food. They laughed at their bootleg reception, with no one attending but them. It was unique and creative; most of all, it was full of joy. Sheaba wished that night would have never ended; it was the best day of her life, and she would not have changed it.

Now they were married, but it was a secret they kept from her family and his, and that was a hard thing for her. He made her promise to wait to tell everyone, but she was so excited about it and did not see the significance of waiting. He thought that it was so sudden, he did not want to shock people with it. Sheaba's conviction caused her to inform her children first and then her pastor and first lady of her former church in Alabama. She felt she owed it to them to tell them the secret. They seemed happy for her, but it all felt wrong in the pit of Sheaba's stomach. She loved them so much and had never meant to hurt them. Her lack of understanding of the shepherd's job to protect his sheep eliminated the responsibility to their care toward her.

Jack was now uncomfortable because nothing had gone as he had planned it. He was not happy that she did not wait and did not trust him and his decision. Just as she thought it would, her soul became sorrowful for the decision she made, and began to have feelings of regret. Hurting people was not something she intentionally set out to do. It was very important for her to keep everyone around her happy. Unfortunately, she failed.

Sheaba hoped that Jack would get past the fact that she had spilled the beans about their marriage too early, as she needed his love to keep her on her toes. She hoped that she had him, even if she had no one else. Her job as an Administrative Assistant at the law firm consumed her; she worked the third shift for five days a week. Third shift had always been her preferred shift, but this time it was harder because she had someone to go home to. All she thought about while at work was lying next to her husband. He made it a point to keep in touch with her every night while at work; sometimes talking to her throughout her shift or on break, depending on the workload for each day. One day something changed and Sheaba was worried.

Sheaba never obtained a key to the house after they married; he would always make excuses. One evening, Jack did not call Sheaba throughout her shift, nor was she able to get in touch with him. When she got off work that morning, she tried calling again, but still, no answer. It was still dark outside when she got home and she was standing outside of the building trying to get into the building that he owned. He had two tenants at the time, and one of them he exclaimed was a female friend. Sheaba never thought she would feel inferior to another woman, as Jack had never given her a reason. But this particular day, after several attempts to get Jacks attention, throwing rocks at his bedroom window and then tapping on it with a tree branch, but still, no answer. By this time, she is worried and wondering if he is ok or just sleeping fairly hard.

Suddenly, Sheaba saw a shadow moving on the second level and hoped it was someone leaving the building so she could get in. It was the lady friend tenant, but she refused to let her in, even after she explained she was married to the landlord. The woman stood blocking the entrance of the door for at least five minutes before she moved out of Sheaba's way. Sheaba caught the door of the entryway of the building before it shut and climbed the short stack of stairs to Jack's apartment. On her way up the stairs she had seen Jack standing their waiting to great her, but it was totally awkward how he did it. Jack said, "Hey! I see you met my tenant." Sheaba looked at him and then walked pass him silently and with disgust. At this point, Sheaba's legs were trembling in fear. Her mind was filled with visions of infidelity that may have happened between the female friend tenant and her husband, Jack. Sheaba thought, *I remember Jack mentioning a while back when we were just having phone conversations as friends that he and the tenant liked one another at one point, but nothing came of it, so they just flirted with one another. He also mentions all they ever did was hug.* They appeared very close when she moved in, as they would talk on the phone almost every day and they always looked out for each other's packages from freight services and mail that came to the building. The tenant and Jack also exchanged food dishes with one another prior to he and Sheaba getting together. That was fine, but it did not appear to be a genuine friendship relationship after she and Jack married. Jack's daughter also had a relationship with the tenant. Jack did not share the same relationship with his male tenant, neither did he develop that kind of relationship with his new tenants when they had come. Sheaba's whole world was crushed as she immediately drew in her mind that Jack and his tenant had relations that night while she was working.

Sheaba immediately and silently climbed into bed to rest her mind and body, and Jack followed. Everything he said to her in his defense felt like a lie; there was nothing he could say to make her believe nothing had happened. Jack said, "I know how this may seem, but I can assure you that nothing ever happened between us! I know if the shoe were on the other foot, I would feel the same way too." Sheaba kept quiet, but the tears began to roll down her face. She cried herself to sleep; if Jack was still talking to her, she did not hear him. Trust was removed from her heart, and anger took its place. The next morning, Jack still wanted to discuss the happenings of earlier that day. Sheaba said: "Jack, I love you, and I forgive you, but it is going to take some time for me to trust you again." I feel like you violated our vows in such a short time of our marriage. Even though you say nothing happened, I feel like it did. I have gone through this before, and my gut says it happened. Not to mention, she had never left for work any day that I have come home from work. We had never crossed paths until today. How ironic." Jack tried to defend himself, but Sheaba could not shake it; nothing he said was believable. From that day forward, their marriage went downhill—and it was not even three months into their marriage. Hell, wreaked havoc in their marriage from that point on; it was as if neither of the two could rekindle what they had.

Jack created a laundry list of how she had changed his heart toward the marriage. Sheaba was pushed to yelling at the top of her lungs at him. Cursing at him and calling him many names to break down his manhood as she had always done in the past when a man hurt her She was so angry that she wanted to physically hurt him bad. The enemy had gotten his hooks into her flesh and prevented her from having a desire to pray to her God. Sheaba felt all that she had learned in therapy with God was thrown out the window, and everything in her past she worked hard to let go was returning. She yelled, "God, help me and my marriage!" The act of retaliation entered her mind and the devil used it to his benefit. He played with her mind so much so that she began to have visions of how she could make him feel the same level of pain. Nevertheless, because she is spiritually connected to God, her soul would not allow her to carry out such acts. For the first time, she understood spiritual warfare and spirits in high places. It felt like she was living in hell; everything failed that Sheaba and Jack tried to do to right the wrong. When Jack tried to show Sheaba how much he loved her, she rejected him, and Jack did the same thing to her afterwards. Sheaba could not trust Jack, but she did not show any insecurity, nor did she pressure him anymore about the situation. However, Jack continued his relationship with the tenant as a friend. The tenant called Jack almost every day to assist her with getting out of being stuck in the snow in front of the building as she was trying to park. Jack and Sheaba would always be spending quality time when it happened and she would interrupt, causing Sheaba to become even less trusting of the two. That is why Sheaba rejected Jacks acts of love toward her. He blatantly showed that she was more important; whenever she called and needed something from him, he would drop everything to do it. That trend kept going for about a year. Sheaba hated Jack so much so that she pushed hard to get him to fight her so she can get him locked up. Jack was smart, he would not touch her, but he tried hard to push past her to get away from her, but she was strong. All she wanted him to do is listen to her feelings about the marriage; he had cut her down negatively explaining how he felt about her. The minute she started talking, he said he did not want to hear it because her tone was too loud. But his voice was loud enough for the neighbors to hear him. He would always do that when Sheaba began responding about her feelings of disappointment toward him. Sheaba kept pushing Jack in his chest, and she pushed him in the face. He called the police and had Sheaba escorted out of the house. He told the police she punched him in the face and scratched his face up. He did have one scratch on his cheek, but she had never punched him. That made her hate him even more. The cops believed him, and she was furious. Luckily, Sheaba's son lived in the apartment next door, the one he wanted her to stay in when she first moved there, but it was not conducive for living. Her son worked hard at getting the apartment to a comfortable living space. The very next day, Sheaba and her son went to Jack's apartment and packed her things. Sheaba's best friend Sheila drove down to help her move back to Alabama. They could not get it right, no matter how hard they tried. Sheaba felt as if Jack had manipulated her from the beginning and she was foolish enough to fall into it. He knew all of her weak moments with men as she talked too much. Sheaba was too honest about her life and men always used her story to see her as gullible. Jack hated Sheaba as well. He said he knew Sheaba was interested in other men and he was never her true choice. He never trusted Sheaba after she accused him of sleeping with his tenant. Six months later, they were divorced.

CHAPTER 5

Relational After-effects

Sheaba moved back home to Alabama after many catastrophic events that propelled her hatred toward Jack, yet her heart still beat for him. Bitterness and embarrassment lived in her soul and tried at every chance to oppress her. Her life was hell; all she wanted to do was hide and never be seen by the world. Her mind played many ugly scenarios of her life every day. At times she would try to reach out to Jack, hoping they could resolve what had happened and rebuild their friendship. That never turned out well. Jack always found a way to insult her character. She tried to remain calm, but as usual, she began to meet him where he was, and she shot verbal bombs at his manhood. She was broken; a fight rose up great within her and the desire to execute it burned in the depths of her belly.

Sheaba's mind slipped into that pathetic state that she remembered from when she was growing up and had spilled into her adulthood. Everything that happened was her fault, as she could have handled everything better if she had allowed God to have his way and had not depended on her emotions. She remembered all that she had done in her marriage. Sheaba tore down her husband's foundation as a man. Her blatant disrespect toward Jack was never forgiven. She attacked Jack every time she felt like he was trying to hurt her indirectly with things he knew she did not like. She did not care if it were in front of people. She demeaned him and made light of things that he took seriously. What was important to him was stupid and immature to Sheaba; he was petty and unforgiving, and there was no reason for her to give him what he wanted. Emotions had always kicked her tail, and it had happened consistently in her life. When she was in the household with him she hated to see him coming home. His presence always put her in a bad mood; thoughts of harming him felt good, but that was out of her character, at least her adulthood character.

Every morning and every night Sheaba went before God, wailing and proclaiming peace in her heart and mind. The situation that went down in her marriage caused her to feel suicidal. Failed relationships is what Sheaba experienced often and she was fed up with it. Her hope in her second marriage was to model a relational example for her children. When that failed, she believed that she failed her children. They had no one in the family to model before them how to handle romantic and marriage relationships appropriately. They voiced that to Sheaba prior to getting married the second time and she thought she married the right man to model that for them, which is why she considered suicide. Suicide was no longer a thought, but an action; she carried it out drinking vodka and swallowing four pills that soldiers typically take for PTSD. The combination of the two impaired her vision, voice, and her limbs; she was found passed out on the bathroom floor, where it appeared she was there at least for an hour before noticed. Sheaba was able to hear everything, but unresponsive; music was playing loudly while Jack and his daughter laughed and enjoyed a good time. Jack eventually found her, had his daughter make a pallet on the bedroom floor, dragged her from the bathroom, down the hall to the bedroom and left her there. Sheaba urinated on herself and puked; her body still did not allow her to move. By the time Sheaba was able to move and see, she was soiled; her body was too weak to get up and clean herself up or get into bed. The room was pitch black, but she saw a shadow of Jack laying in the bed and heard him snoring. The next morning Sheaba was a little bit stronger than before, she cleaned herself up and for two days recouped.

The next morning Sheaba asked Jack why he did not call the ambulance and why he left her on the floor with the mice and roaches. His response was, "I am a marine, I knew I did not need the paramedics, you were fine. Sheaba never believed Jack hurt at all about anything that he did to her or cared enough to make attempts to fix the marriage. He was great at showing no mercy to those who he believed was hurting him. Jack's retaliation was always worse than Sheaba could handle, and he did not care about the tears she shed. Even when they were in the same room, he would act like she was not there. Releasing all those thoughts to God didn't seem to be helping, but she did her best by speaking them out loud to God whatever she was thinking and feeling inside. She was a raging bull that was about to burst. *Lord, help my thoughts*, she said. *You did not allow me to die, so now what would you have me to do. My husband is out of control and I do not know what to do anymore. I want out.*

Her self-esteem was at rock bottom, and it trapped her between the walls of her past and present. Jack and Sheaba had no intimacy, she could count on both of her hands how many times he touched her the two years they had been married. Every day she woke up feeling like she had no right to be alive. The war in her body was real, and no one would ever understand how deep the rage was within. Everyone had their own agenda and needed to care for themselves. To pour her burdens on her friends and family only caused shame, guilt, and pain. Instead, she journeyed alone in her sorrows. As she entered into her wilderness experience, God met her where she was, as he always did.

Climbing Out of the Wilderness

Instead of Sheaba whining to God about what she had gone through those past few years, she reminded herself of the therapeutic journey with God as a guide toward a reasonable recovery. God had built her from nothing to something; he had spoken life into her and created a strong foundation, but Sheaba had always found a way to add ungodly things to her foundation, causing it to be shaken. It was not always intentional; the temptations were real and easily attainable. Living for God was not easy; desire was always lurking somewhere each time God shared his love. A man of flesh is who she would turn to, hoping to find the love God was giving her in him. Although she believed she was healed after a year of her divorce with Jack, she realized quickly that she would always be hunted by the temptation and desire to have a man of flesh. God had never set Sheaba up to fail, she failed because of impatience. Her wilderness experience was designed to re-build the foundation that was shattered when she married Jack the first time. In the wilderness, Sheaba learned that everything that she had seen from her natural eye-site or heard from her natural way of hearing was not good. Not everything that was presented before her was healthy for her foundation in God. Sheaba was reminded of the story in the Bible where God presented a tree in the middle of the garden and told Adam and Eve that though it was good to look upon, it never was to be touched. Sheaba recognized that the same was presented in her world, but with diverse temptations. God did not have to tell her not to touch the forbidden; she knew prior to marrying Jack, in their first negative encounter that she had violated God's directive. The convictions she felt after that first humiliating visit with Jack, was God's chastisement—but she did not heed the warning. Sheaba did not see it that way and continued to pursue the relationship with Jack. One old saying she heard people saying about God stood out in her mind like a sore thumb: "God works in mysterious ways!" If nothing else was true, that statement was.

Prior to the divorce, Sheaba remembered that since she had chosen to enter the forbidden place, God was holding her accountable for living a Godly life before her husband, despite his actions toward her. If she had allowed herself more time with God instead of allowing her emotions to drive, she would have learned, through the word of God, how to be a submissive and loving wife. Her marriage to God was compromised through her failing test of commitment. Jack had become her priority rather than God, so she married him. Sheaba thought God had provided Jack to her because of what appeared to be marital bliss the day of their wedding at the courthouse. It was nothing like her first marriage where God warned her at the altar to withdraw. Before Jack had come along she was enjoying what God provided in her single life. However, the enemy fooled her as he did Eve in the garden of Eden (Genesis 3 KJV); he presented Jack as a loving and selfless man. Satan knew he could push her to feed her addiction. In Sheaba's guilt, she, as usual, accepted fault for the divorce. Her theory was, she went into a relationship and a marriage as a mature woman of God, who had the power, wisdom and knowledge to win her husband over with Godly love; yet she allowed her fleshly emotions to overtake her mind and body, and fought fire with fire. It was too late to change, Jack had already started a war that forced their marriage to a bitter end.

Jack was not serving God, but he would attend church services with Sheaba. He had often told her that he was going for himself and not for her. At that moment, Sheaba thought, *just maybe our marriage will take a turn for the best since he is trying God.* Though Jack attempted to begin to learn how to live for God, Sheaba knew it would take time before the true headship from God would resonate with Jack. As Sheaba was learning to live Godly before Jack, her flesh crawled when she had to be nice to him whenever he blatantly disrespected her or offended. After doing it often, she could feel the joy of the Lord released in her heart toward Jack. Her upside-down smile turned upright, the pain from disrespect and offense was channeled toward God so she could do it again, and again, until Jack realized it did no longer phased her.

At first, when Sheaba went into battle on her knees for her marriage, she refused to be committed to the cause God called her to when things got tough; that is to love despite of offence. To do things her way felt better because it showed her strength. Unleashing her fiery darts on Jack was supposed to prove to him that she was not weak. It was supposed to teach Jack never to manipulate or attack her in any way or to expect to win easily. However, Jack showed Sheaba that she was the weaker vessel against him. He was a beast in heart and as stubborn as a mule. She could not compete with that, as she was trying to mask her sensitivity with aggression. *What did I think I would accomplish? Why did I believe I could fight against a military man in my fleshly strength? Sheaba thought.* Sheaba smiled as she accepted accountability and defeat. Though it hurt, for the first time she did not point the finger at her offender and accuser. God always had a way with teaching how to judge oneself and shows how things could have been done differently.

> Judge not that ye be not judged. For with what judgment ye judge, ye shall be judged: and with what measure ye mete, it shall be measured to you again. And why beholdest thou the mote that is in thy brother's eye, but considerest not the beam that is in thine own eye? (Matthew 7:1-3 KJV)

> Examine yourselves, to see whether you are in the faith. Test yourselves. Or do you not realize this about yourselves, that Jesus Christ is in you? Unless indeed you fail to test! (2 Corinthians 13:5).

Sheaba was pained to recognize that so many has wasted time trying to find happiness and had been hurt in the process. Personalities intertwined outside of the divine order of God, and there were shattered dreams and hopes. The music of love was only from God, and when he was not involved, it stopped playing. Every chord was out of tune, and its sound was distorted by the voices of negative emotions. The air became polluted with a smell that sickened purged bellies, which forced untruthful illusions. Although God previously had begun her purging process, she had been rejecting it unnoticeably. Unintentionally, she allowed herself to be caught up in lies she told herself— "I cannot do this!" "It is too hard to accomplish!" "I will never get it right!" "I love men so much; I do not think I can let go long enough to receive God's promises!" She kept letting go of God's hand the minute man's love sang songs to her heart and mind. God showed her his love, which was always embedded deep inside, but in her humanity and lack of wisdom, she equated that with fleshly love. In her therapy sessions, God specifically pointed out the difference between his love and human love; a unified bond was not present in the way she found and experienced love with her own kind, but transient love that eventually fades away when its expectations are not met.

God gave Sheaba a dose of reality when he took her hand in marriage. He challenged her femininity and commitment. When she failed, he gave her man and told her to love him despite his flaws. It was then she realized there was no real love in her flesh that epitomizes God's unfeigned love. No man could give Sheaba the exact love as God. Only a man that was after God's heart could love as he does. He poured so much love upon her that it felt as if the desire for man dissipated. She did not serve a selfish God but one who desired everyone to obtain his love and share it.

> Hereby perceive we the love of God, because he laid down
> his life for us; and we ought to lie down our lives for the
> brethren. (1 John 3:16 KJV).

Sheaba decided from the day of her divorce from Jack that she would love and forgive according to the way God taught her to do so. In addition, she would make provision to give up fighting in any way. That is physically, verbally, emotionally, however a fight can be acted out, she was going to die to it. Although, it would bring pain to her flesh physically, and her heart emotionally, she believed it was the right thing to do. To deal with people who loves retaliation, were unforgiving, manipulative, and liars, was suicide, and Sheaba was about to make herself vulnerable to it all. In her vulnerability, the love of God would infiltrate her negative emotions and create a new life and new beginnings, and that was what she had been striving so hard to obtain.

Sheaba started by lifting her hands, opening her mouth, and releasing despair and defeat; declaring that she would yield her tongue, thoughts, and her limbs to God, to prevent any and all aggressive behavior. In the process of her declaration, she felt a strong presence of God that knocked her off her feet. Her stomach twisted in knots, her head began to throb, and her eyes burned as if she had hot coals placed on them. Lying on the floor, she accepted that her life with Christ would be served differently and she would no longer succumb to her worldly flesh. Regardless of how society would look at her, she would wait on God before she made any decisions on her next move toward a romantic relationship or marriage. Any truth about her life would no longer be a secret, God and the world would see her as an open book, which will prevent the enemy from attempting to embarrass or torment. Sheaba definitely did not want God to expose her hidden secrets, therefore she always prayed to him in spirit and in truth.

The fight within her was on; there was no more pretending or keeping secrets that would haunt her in the future. Sheaba decided to never straddle the fence; never to deny God or be embarrassed of the life she had chosen with him. Satan was not going to save her from the trauma life she lived, only God, her Father in heaven. This was her first step in learning to walk upright before God by faith. In her heart, she believed that everyone had a different relationship with God. This was Sheaba's way of working out her own salvation with fear and trembling. On that day, she developed a covenant with God and started a new relationship in *truth*.

CHAPTER 6

After the Storm

A New Mind and New Direction

When Sheaba returned home to Alabama, she moved in with her daughter Dalia until she could find a job. Prior to Sheaba's divorce Jack encouraged her to give her truck to her daughter since they had more than one car already. Neither car was in Sheaba's name, therefore after the divorce she was left with no car. Things were a lot harder without a car to get around to search for work and a new home. Her thoughts played back the events that took place prior to her divorce. It still hurt her soul to have lost her husband. Sheaba felt, to believe that divorce was supposed to happen to them was to believe their existence was a lie. Divorce was never something she agreed with; there had to be a fight to stay in her marriage rather than running away from it. Unfortunately, she was the only one fighting.

Although God took her through the test of commitment, she never expected that he would bring the two together only to break them apart. Sheaba realized afterwards, her marriage was out of the alignment of God; however, she definitely believed God had given her Jack. Her marriage was dysfunctional because her dysfunction intertwined with Jack's dysfunction. God had not yet completed either of their purging process. If it were meant for the two to be together things would have been close to perfect. Sheaba knows when God is in anything, it works out as he plans it. Sheaba thought her relationship going into the marriage, and the wedding that happened at the courthouse was perfect; they both had an amazing experience. After everything was said and done, trauma almost started immediately. Once before the romantic relationship started and later within the first three months of marriage. God had warned Sheaba, but she missed the mark.

Before Sheaba moved in with Dalia, she stayed one night with her best friend Serita. That first night back home, she got extremely sick. It was not like her to be hurling all over the place. Her body shivered as if the house had no heat, but sweat beads framed her forehead. Serita cleaned up the mess Sheaba made and covered her with a thick blanket; then she gave her water and a plastic bag, in case she had the urge to hurl again. Serita called Sheaba's daughter Dalia to let her know her mother was sick and to confirm a time she would be picking her up in the morning, as she had to work and did not want to leave her alone.

All of the nervous energy she had encountered gave way to stress, which took over her body; she needed rest. The remainder of the night Sheaba slept peacefully; it seemed as if she had never rested when she was with Jack; she was always on edge. The next morning Dalia showed up two hours after Serita left. Sheaba was still sick and silent during the drive to her daughter's house. Dalia's apartment was small, so Sheaba hung out mostly in the living room. After Dalia made room for all of Sheaba's things, they sat and talked for a little bit but nothing regarding her personal life. Sheaba relaxed the entire day sleeping off and on while trying to watch a little television.

The next morning when Dalia went to work, Sheaba had the house to herself. It was the perfect moment to spend time with God. Feeling hopeless and helpless, she talked to God about her feelings and where she was mentally. Sharing everything that was deep in her soul with God made her feel great, so she always did it, and she made sure she was honest. She left nothing out and allowed God to deal with every level of her insecurities and instabilities.

The living room was a bit gloomy, as the blinds were closed, but during her talk with God, the sun shined so brightly that it lit up the room. Sheaba had always considered that was God's approval of her prayers. When she opened the blinds, her phone rang; it was a friend from church, offering her a position at her Daycare and School. The position was to start as an Executive Assistant with a possibility to be promoted if she did well the first year. The job started immediately, so she prepared herself mentally and physically for the next day.

When Dalia came home from work, she told her of the good news, and they both went out to celebrate over dinner. They laughed and talked about how good God is and then left to make sure Sheaba had enough time to prepare herself for her new job. That next morning was bitterly cold, and the buses were very slow. While waiting for the bus, she listened to the music on her google play playlist. A song played that pricked her soul and raised her spirits. The song was called, "Made a Way" by Travis Greene. Sheaba played the song over and over until she made it to work. Every day she repeated that song; it gave her hope that everything would be alright; that she had overcome, and God had led her all the way. As she faced her pain with the joy of that song, the joy of the lord began healing her on the inside. Instead of her showing pain outwardly, joy illuminated from the inside on the outside. To express joy in her pain was different, but it felt like a new lease on life.

The song resonated in her spirit so strong that she found herself worshipping and praising God while on the bus, something she had never done before. She held her hands high in the air with tears rolling down her face. She could feel people starring at her, but she paid them no mind; all she cared about was the healing she was receiving through the presence of God.

It was great being back home. Returning to her home church was the best, even though she hurt some feelings with her leaving before, they all welcomed her back with open arms. Sheaba knew it was not the right time to return to her old duties at the church, she wanted to wait until God revealed that the timing was right. The more important task was to apologize to her leaders for her sudden leave and not allowing them time to bless me and my future endeavors. They were responsible for her soul, yet she left them no room to honor her leave and make sure she was going into safe hands. The way she left them had been rude; it had showed immaturity, especially since she had been spiritually raised by them. They had walked hand in hand with Sheaba from the beginning of her walk with Christ and had never left her side.

Doing the right thing was always what Sheaba wanted to do, but when it had come to making decisions about being with a man, it was hard. Sheaba set up a meeting after service with the Pastor and his wife, where she apologized again, and made a promise, with sincerity, to never make a sudden move like that again, and she declared that she would give proper notice. They were great leaders and also great mentors who always understood and forgave. They loved Sheaba and only had her best interest, spiritually and naturally, at hand. Slowly, she got back to doing things for the first lady and the church. Nothing was better than serving God and his people; it was Sheaba's passion.

Six months had gone by, and things were going well, naturally, and spiritually. Sheaba received a promotion on the job and was able to purchase another vehicle. Sheaba was thankful to God for where she was at that moment; she never ceased studying the Bible daily and praying. Communicating with God made her feel safe, happy, and at peace. Already, she had forgiven Jack for the trauma she experienced in her marriage. She continued to work on loving, in spite of how people treated her. That was one of the hardest tasks in her walk with God, as people always tried taking advantage of others wherever possible. Sheaba tried not to anticipate the pain that she would encounter living without aggression or retaliation. That was how she protected herself for many years, however, it only made life miserable. As she fought with her innermost thoughts, Jack had come to mind. *To make amends with Jack would be awesome, but how would that look?* she thought.

Sheaba was far from interested in rekindling their relationship, but at least they could put an end to the enemy's plight to hate. The love she had for Jack was unlike what she had for any man, and that was not going anywhere. It was just too bad things turned out the way they did. Sulking about it was not going to change anything. Sheaba thought, *I should have given Jack to God* (*that meant to leave him in the hands of God*) *in the beginning, and it was not a bad idea to do it now.* How great it made her feel to finally see and handle things differently. No longer did she have her guard up, ready to attack every issue with a vengeance or even to defend her honor on things that others accused her of doing wrong to them. Taking things to God was her only defense; it helped her to be at ease, knowing he would reveal right and wrong. Not only that, but he taught her how to handle being right or wrong and how not to exude arrogance or self-pity. After all, being right or wrong never brought happiness, and it certainly was not a way to breed love.

If Sheaba knew anything, she knew that the God she served could do everything. Whatever God was a part of became a success. What she had experienced six months ago was her past; she had learned from it and had been given another chance to climb out of the wilderness.

The Awkward Antipathy

After being apart for six months, Sheaba decided to call Jack to see how he was doing. As usual, he did not answer the phone, but that was okay. A few minutes later, he called back. The first thing he asked was if everything was okay. Shocked by the question, she paused and then said yes. There wasn't much to talk about, so she told Jack the phone call was just to see how he was doing and to see if he was able to forgive her. He was still harping on how she accused him of cheating. The awkwardness of where the conversation was leading caused Sheaba's stomach to do flips.

Calmly, she listened to the same stuff he harped at her during their marriage. When he was done, she tried to speak, but he cut her off. Then she cut him off, and he got really angry. Sheaba felt bad, as she did not expect the phone call to go that way. She hoped he would say that he had missed her and that they both had been wrong, but that was not going to happen. That was the day she accepted that there will never be a change in his mind about the negative events in their marriage. Sheaba thanked Jack for returning the call and promised she would never bother him again. He agreed and hung up.

Although Sheaba felt as if she had forgiven Jack, after that phone call, it was noticed that she still had not forgiven him for how he had treated her and the accusations he made against her. However, she knew forgiving Jack would get rid of all those negative emotions so she could move on. Staying away from him a bit longer would definitely help strengthen her stance if she had to talk with Jack again. Jack was too much to handle; he fought about everything, and there was nothing he would not debate. If he did not win the conversation, he would begin insulting. His insults were subtle, so he could justify he was not doing that. He would blame Sheaba for being overly sensitive and unable to handle a debate. Sheaba had always told him she was not the type to debate, as it always felt like an argument, but he would always force her into a debate of some sort. The fact that she no longer had to deal with that, made her very happy.

That evening Sheaba thought about what transpired earlier with Jack and the feeling she had experienced. Desiring to be rid of the feeling, she went before God and expressed what was inside. In detail, she gave God all that she was feeling toward Jack. It was her hope that God would lead her to scriptures that will teach her true forgiveness and how to apply it. For the next six months, Sheaba added Jack to her prayers and forgiveness.

In her studies, she read, "Let all bitterness, and wrath, and anger, and clamour, and evil speaking, be put away from you, with all malice: and be ye kind one to another, tenderhearted, forgiving one another, even as God for Christ's sake hath forgiven you" (Ephesians 4:31–32 KJV). In that, she learned it was important first to be purged from her own evilness and not worry about Jack's issues. It was important for her to learn how to keep quite when offence had come and learn not to apply the evil things spoken toward her. The only way she could win that battle was to talk to Jack or be around him, and she knew just how to accomplish that.

Sheaba's oldest son, Ernest, lived next door to Jack; that would have been excuse enough to visit, but she refused to use her son to complete her task. Unfortunately, she was forced to go to the building to care for her son who had been in and out of the hospital for various reasons. However, Jack and Sheaba never crossed paths during that time. One evening she was visiting, and Jack knocked on the door after Ernest went to the store.

When Sheaba answered the door, Jack said, "Hello." "Hi," said Sheaba. Smiling, she asked, "How can I assist you?" "Is Ernest here? I'd like to speak with him." "No, he left a few minutes ago to go to the store. I will let him know you came by." "Ok! Thank you." He stood at the door after his response. Awkwardly, Sheaba said, "I like the color you dyed your beard, you look very nice. Are you heading out somewhere tonight? He smiled and said, "Thank you! No, not at all. I am just trying something new. I actually had just gotten home."

Finally, he decided to go back to his apartment, and Sheaba hurriedly shut the door. She took a deep breath, as she wanted to hug him. She felt how much she loved him and did not want to hide it. Ernest returned shortly thereafter; she told him that Jack had come by, and he immediately went over. Ernest never shared why Jack wanted to see him, and he never would tell me. He always stayed out of our mess, as he had his own problems to deal with. Besides, he loved both of them and did not want to be in the middle of their pain. Sheaba stayed overnight and drove back home in the morning after cleaning Ernest's apartment, making sure he took his meds, and ate.

On the drive home, Sheaba's mind went in many directions. Immediately, she yielded those thoughts to God to help her still her thoughts. Her mixed emotions would do nothing but cause confusion and negativity. Here is what God dropped in her spirit:

> The weapons of our warfare are not carnal, but mighty
> through God to the pulling down of strongholds, casting

down imaginations and every thought that exalteth itself against the knowledge of God, and bringing into captivity every thought unto the obedience of Christ. (2 Corinthians 10:4-5)

Peace I leave with you, my peace I give unto you: not as the world giveth, give I unto you. Let not your heart be troubled, neither let it be afraid. (John 14:27 KJV)

That put a smile on her face, so she turned on some upbeat gospel music and boogied all the way home. Later that night, Jack called, but she did not answer, as she was already overwhelmed by the surprise visit. He left a message to let her know the last puppy they raised had passed on. Instead of returning the call, she thanked him through text for letting her know, and said she would keep him in prayer.

Before the divorce, Sheaba had raised four blue nose pit bulls from birth; they were stolen from their backyard, and only one of them was found. Her heart was broken, and it took several weeks for her to get over it. It bothered her so much that she had several dreams that moved her to tears. Losing the last puppy was hurtful but not as bad because she was not there when it happened.

One year later, Ernest decided to move out of Jack's building in Champaign and back to Alabama. Sheaba drove down to help, as did Ernest's older brother Clayton. Clayton was born to Sheaba's children father and another woman, but he was very much her son as well. She loved Clayton as if he were her own. Ernest rented a U-Haul, and everyone helped load it, including Jack's daughter's boyfriend and two of his friends. After everything was out of the apartment, everyone sat outside of the building, talking. Jack came out to say goodbye to Ernest and was introduced to his big brother. Sheaba sat in the U-Haul, as she was over heated and had a really bad headache. Looking through the side-view mirror, she saw Jack walking toward the truck, so she let the window down.

They chatted respectfully, which was a bit awkward again, but it turned out to be great conversation. There was no talk of the past. He mostly spoke about his new direction toward Christ. Shockingly to her, he had kept his promise and continued going to church. While sharing a few funny stories about his debates in one of the men's ministries at the church he attended, Ernest broke up the conversation, as he was ready to leave. Jack said it had been time well spent, and Sheaba agreed. Jack hugged Sheaba, kissed her on the cheek, and waved goodbye. The drive home was great. She had no preconceived thoughts of what had occurred, nor did she feel any negative emotions. Sheaba had just experienced forgiveness without a word spoken about it, but she wanted to know for sure that she truly had forgiven him. It did not matter to her if Jack forgave her, as she left that to God.

It was fulfilling to hear that Jack was allowing God to resuscitate him under the guidance of the Word of truth. Jack made every effort to learn who God is and what God desired for his life. He was being rebirthed and washed in the blood of the lamb. Jack mentioned that throughout his journey, he was learning more about himself and his struggles everyday. He listened to the voice of God and recognized God's hand in his life. Although he still struggled with forgiveness, he fought for truth to dwell within; that was his desire.

Sheaba found herself in a place of silence. She believed God wanted her to hear and not be heard. She prayed often and continued to seek God for clarity of his Word during devotional time. She did not know where she stood with God in her new life's journey, but she pressed forward daily to get closer to him so she could closely hear his voice and be clear of his direction. Spiritual silence assisted Sheaba with hearing what the Lord has to say and allowing her to be aware of her surroundings. Silence helped Sheaba to make better decisions and less prone to being fooled by the enemy. Also, God would clarify her gifts and how he wanted her to operate in them.

God knew she had a habit of hearing and not listening; if she were listening, she would carry out his commands. Although Sheaba made multiple mistakes and bad decisions, her love for God never ceased. Despite all that happened within those years before and after divorce,

Sheaba and Jack were okay. God worked on both of them. They did not talk often, but they stayed in contact here and there, a little bit.

Sheaba declared to God that she would commit her bones, organs, and ligaments to adhere to the sound of God's voice. She declared that if she ever turned her back on God, she would surely experience physical death; the breath of life would exit her body. That was how much she loved God and refused to leave him again to esteem man above him. Her new life was the best she had ever experienced. She was happy and more in tune with herself, and in love with God. To understand her direction and know more about what makes her tick, was the best feeling in the world.

CHAPTER 7

⁛ 𝕊𝕡 ⁛

Recommitting to God's Love

The Purge

Sheaba fell in love on several occasions but found herself digging through trenches of cement to have it reciprocated. She was stuck in the thorns of her past, which caused excruciating pain as she tried to pry herself out. Taking deep breaths through her mouth was important, as doing it through her nose caused her joints to lock up from taking in undeserving depression in the air. Feeling ensnared and resentful, Sheaba always scurried to a place of solitude for recovery.

In her hiding place, and silent prayer, she made contact with the sound of a soft but authoritative voice that alarmed her conscience and awakened her soul: "I love you. Come to me, and I will give you rest." The music from Sheaba's heart was a strong drumbeat that was so loud that she was sure it could be heard from a distance. Again, the voice spoke, only a little bit louder: "I love you. Cast your cares upon me. I won't leave you alone."

Perspiration poured down her face, and her eyes burned like hot coals had been applied to them. It felt like needles were poking into her cheeks, almost like bee stings. The question in her mind was, *Is God proposing to me again?* Instead of meeting her, as before, in depression, he met her at a point of condemnation. Unlike previously,

Sheaba's body responded quickly to the thick, spiritual atmosphere. Sheaba was always sensitive to the Spirit of God, but somehow she found ways to fight it when she wanted things to go her way.

God began filling her once-empty stomach with love and wisdom. Her mind stood still, and she had no thoughts of her own. Patiently, she waited for God's anointing to calm her pulsating temples. Standing humbly in the presence of God, Sheaba was ready to receive the seed of Christ. She carried his child once and had miscarried due to her inconsistency and commitment issues. She was excited about the new seed that was being planted in her womb, and she relaxed her body to receive him appropriately.

As Sheaba lie still and calm, a new flow of tears slid down her cheeks and cured the burns from the earlier tears and soothed the heat of her burning eyes. *He loves me still*, Sheaba thought. Only the touch of God could heal her internally and externally; he was her perfect covering.

As God covered Sheaba with words of affirmation, she felt a sense of belonging. He wanted her and her alone. She could come to him authentic; without hiding the real person. He claimed her and was willing to be by her side. He created her to love him, even though she did not understand that kind of love. God was taking the time to show her how to love him, as she submitted time with him. He wanted Sheaba to know he is the author of everything and being committed to him makes her an heir of all things.

> All things were made by him; and without him was not anything made that was made. (John 1:3 KJV)

> And now, I entrust you to God and the message of his grace that is able to build you up and give you an inheritance with all those he has set apart for himself. (Romans 8:17 NLT)

No one loved her more than her Father in heaven. It took Sheaba countless years to own up to the fact that there was none who could love at the depth of God. Her heart melted, knowing despite her disobedience, sinfulness, unrighteousness, whoremongering, and deceitfulness, God put a bid in for her. He counted her as worthy among many who deemed her unworthy. He tolerated the stench of her flesh and washed her until a sweet-smelling aroma burst from her pours into thin air and awakened her consciousness. "Greater love hath no man than this, that a man lay down his life for his friends." (John 15:3 KJV) That scripture sang songs of love to her spirit and she did not want to let go.

He went on further to reassure her, adding melody to the song saying, "Scarcely for a righteous man will one die, yet peradventure for a good man some would even dare to die. But God commanded his love toward us, in that, while we were yet sinners, Christ died for us. Much more then, being now justified by his blood, we shall be saved from wrath through him" (Romans 5:7–9 KJV).

Sheaba's love for God was insurmountable. Although her flesh always warred against the love she had for God, she would fight to the best of her ability to die to it. No longer did the desire for man overpower her love and desire for God. He was her man; no human man would take her from him again. With feet planted and a grounded soul in God, Sheaba began to hide his Word in her heart. His blood rushed through her veins like ocean waves, which pushed all the toxic waste from it. The power of God's presence caused the hairs on her body to stand at attention, awaiting his instructions. His touch was overwhelmingly great! Her bones locked until they were spoken to. They were unable to move at normal capacity, but when the word of the Lord reached them, it created a lubricant that loosened them all.

At every thought of God, her lips trembled, and her ears gave way to the harmony of his love songs. As her arms raised, her feet began to shuffle, and at every attempt to utter a word, her tongue stiffened. In a matter of seconds, his anointing engulfed her being and forced a language to spill from her loins unlike her own. His sweet love intertwined with her soul, as it did the first time he held her on their first day of marriage. The climax was indefinite, causing her knees to buckle as her body gave in to his commands.

Lying there, she experienced a cool breeze that swept over her body, as if a fan had been turned on, and Sheaba embraced God's charisma, one that assassinated her addiction for men. Her eyes clenched tighter, as she did not want to come down from the spiritual height of where she was in the presence of God; but the coolness forced her to relax. Her lungs expanded, and her chest gave way to normal breaths, and a breath of fresh air, unlike before, opened her eyes to new visions. Her lips spread wide with joy, and a sound of laughter burst from the depths of her belly. She was made a new person. Nothing looked the same. Although the sound of life was the same, the approach had changed. *Oh, how the passion of Christ can change a life*, she thought.

Thoughts of his love kept running through her mind while her body was still quivering in shock. The very essence of God's love had thrust her being into heavenly places. That heavenly place infiltrated her flesh and cleansed her of the sins that infested her body. While her body was relaxed, her dysfunctions were forced to adhere to God's commandments, which ultimately impaired areas of her body that were disobedient. Her hearing was keen, and her eyes began to see the reality of life, which discombobulated her flesh, but made her soul content.

Peace manifested itself in her loins and accepted God's sovereignty. Every inch of her body became apologetic for all that was said, done, or thought that was displeasing to God during her defiant seasons. It was ashamed of what was unveiled. It was Sheaba, the one who had been with several men, who had killed her spiritual baby for a one-night stand and an ounce of love that was not true love. She was the one whose tongue could cause a forest fire and kill every living thing that stood against her.

She was made whole again, and it was an amazing feeling. She and God had rekindled their love and had joined hands in marriage again. It was a pleasure being married to a man who was above all men, who had given her compassion, mercy, love, patience, and, most of all, forgiveness and unmerited grace.

Sheaba finally rose to her feet with limited strength, as the power of God was still upon her. After finding a place to sit, she silently gazed in one direction for several minutes. Before the trance diminished, that soft voice spoke to her consciousness again: "You are mine, and I am yours, and I will be with you until the end of time."

> But this is the covenant that I will make with the house of Israel after those days, declares the Lord; I will put my law within them, and I will write it on their hearts, And I will be their God, and they will be my people. (Jeremiah 31:33 KJV)

The strength in Sheaba's body returned, but everything felt different. *Something has changed*, she thought. Every negative thought that lived in Sheaba's mind had been removed. Her body felt lighter, her heartbeat was normal, and her chest sat upright. Confidence saturated her body and whipped it into shape. With great excitement, Sheaba found herself sharing sweet testimonies of a man who had stolen her heart. Many were excited for her and wanted to meet the man of whom she had spoken of so eloquently. They kept asking his name and wanted information about how and where they had met.

Not a day had gone by where she refused to uphold and esteem him. Being pressed so much, eventually she gave up his name, "Jesus!" They asked, why are you so frustrated? She exclaimed, *I am not frustrated, I am excited to proclaim the name of a man who had stolen my heart.*

Then all the murmuring began. "Oh girl! You told that story like he was real," they said. "I thought you got your groove on."

Sheaba just smiled and told them, *one day you will desire to give up your way of life for a taste of his sweet honey dew. The authenticity of the love of God would overthrow the fictitious and exaggerated love of your men of flesh. I dare any of you to try him, I promise you too will fall head over hills in love with him.*

Sheaba thought, *maybe people thought God had forced himself into her life in her painful and vulnerable moments.* What they did not realize is that it was fortunate that God entered into her welcoming space in those vulnerable moments. He was right on time when she engaged into her quiet time. An intimate relationship began when she poured her heart out before him in prayer with humility. Sheaba felt it would have been foolish not to acknowledge the voice of God. In those moments of her life, it would have caused great detriment to ignore him. But God, who is full of love and grace, touched her and made her whole just when she needed it.

Sheaba believed God knows everything and if he had not met her where she was, her life would have been hopeless. God knew the heart of Sheaba and chose her from the inception of her life. It was Sheaba who needed to acknowledge him to move forward in the relationship.

The Threefold Chord of God

Without the threefold chord of God, her marriage was no good.

> Two are better than one, because they have a good return for their labor: if either of them falls down, one can help the other up. But pity anyone who falls and has no one to help them up. Also, if two lies down together, they will keep warm. But how can one keep warm alone? Though one may be overpowered, two can defend themselves. A cord of three strands is not quickly broken. (Ecclesiastes 4:9–12 NIV)

And it was so. Sheaba understood that only God could hold together any relationship. He is the epitome of love and was teaching Sheaba that love was more than a good feeling. Sheaba thought that love was not supposed hurt, but it tormented her in human relationships. However, God's love spoke volumes to her spirit.

> Love is patient, love is kind. It does not envy, it does not
> boast, it is not proud. It does not dishonor others, it is not
> self-seeking, it is not easily angered, it keeps no record
> of wrongs. Love does not delight in evil but rejoices with
> the truth. It always protects, always trusts, always hopes,
> always preserves. (1 Corinthians 13:4–7 NIV)

Before and after Sheaba married Jack, she believed that scripture applied to them. A few months after marriage, more than one of those attributes took a turn for the worse. When God captured Sheaba, while still in her marriage, he emancipated her with his love. God's love gave her the strength to hold fast to her marriage despite the indirect disrespect and emotional abuse she experienced from Jack. Jack was subtle in extrapolating his evil tactics. He did them in a way that they could not be easily exposed. Jack always wanted to look like a good guy, but even his actions told lies his mouth did not tell. God deposited just enough love into Sheaba to extinguish the fire of Jacks indignation. At times, it made Jack squirm in his chair; he would have this look in his eyes of confusion, wondering how Sheaba was able to relax in the heat. Love did wonders for Sheaba; especially when Jack did everything in his power to make her feel sad and helpless. Love protected Sheaba from depression, it moved fear from her heart, and opened her eyes to truth. What Jack thought she did not know, she knew. God always had a way with revealing things about Jack. He always assumed someone told her, when it was God who had given her the visions and inklings.

One phone call changed their path. Jack allowed conversations that were disrespecting their marriage and then love turned to rage, distrust, and a separation from the third chord. Sheaba was fed up with the blatant disrespect Jack presented. Sheaba asked, "Jack can we talk?" "About what?" said Jack. "Our marriage and how it has been manipulated." said Sheaba. "I don't know what you mean by manipulated. Manipulated by whom?" said Jack. "You Jack!" said Sheaba. Jack laughed and said, "woman relax! Why are you all up in arms?" By now, Sheaba was enraged and could not take no more of his sarcasm and hidden agendas. Before she knew it, she had given up, nothing was working, and it appeared that Jack no longer cared. Sheaba said without fear and with full awareness of how Jack would react, "Do you want a divorce? Because this emotional rollercoaster you are trying to keep me on has been shut down. You give more attention to your tenant, of whom you have been sleeping with, and your ex-girlfriend who calls anytime she feel disrespected by someone or when she think she is being followed by a stranger. Who are you married to, me or them?" Jack responded, "You know what, I am sick of you accusing me. I will go down to the courthouse tomorrow and pick up the papers. We are going to do this immediately." Within a week Jack had the divorce papers in hand and handed them to Sheaba. He said, "we can have this done in one day, just fill them out and together we can go downtown to finish it." Sheaba did not want a divorce, she was hoping Jack would make an effort to find a solution to their problems. Jack said their marriage was a snowball effect and it keeps getting bigger and bigger; there is certainly no resolve.

It was time for Sheaba to put on her boxing gloves; Jack was about to throw punches and she wanted to be ready. She knew how to fight; she was always a good fighter. She fought fair but with understanding and wisdom. She kept her eyes and ears opened at all times and waited for God's instructions to hit hard in unblocked areas. Ducking, dodging, and weaving was something she had never done. Her modus operandi was to block, stick, and move, which helped her win her fights. In this case Sheaba has to duck, dodge, and weave, a new technique that she had never used, therefore, awkwardness made her feel like she would be defeated. But Sheaba refused to allow the devil to win the fight. He was destined to go down, and it was just a matter of time before she would do it.

It looked as though Sheaba was losing. She lost her breath at certain points, and her emotions flared tremendously. Rage seduced her, and her head filled with pain, but God, in his timeliness, gave her a battleground scripture:

> Put on the full armor of god, so that you can take your
> stand against the devil's schemes. (Ephesians 6:11 NIV)

And then he gave her a serenity prayer:

> Create in me a clean heart, O God, and renew a right spirit
> within me. Cast me not away from your presence and take
> not your Holy Spirit from me. Restore to me the joy of your
> salvation and uphold me with a willing spirit. Then I will
> teach transgressors your ways, and sinners will return to
> you. (Psalm 51:10–13 NIV)

Jack needed to feel in control to love; when he did not get it, he attacked Sheaba's happiness. Anything she loved he found a way to sabotage it. She was affectionate, he stopped giving affection to her. She loved when he wore cologne, he stopped wearing it. She loved the puppies he kept for her, he gave them away and made it look as if they were stolen. He stopped talking to her, cooking for her, and giving her intimacy. It hurt at first, but then Sheaba embraced the serenity prayer. Sheaba repeated those scriptures almost daily to keep the spiritual beam in her eyes for her husband, even though it was too late.

In her natural eyes, Jack was evil and ugly; he had no remorse and was selfish and manipulative. Her spiritual eyes saw past the evilness that possessed her husband's spirit, and she stood strong in the armor of God to protect him through showering him with the weapon of love. She knew she rubbed him the wrong way and divorce was already the plan, but she hoped that he would change his mind. Every time Sheaba felt evil raise up in Jack, she would fight to keep the presence of evil from penetrating her body. Gut punching it with the word of truth, she acknowledged the evil spirit, and told it, "No weapon formed against me shall prosper, and every tongue which rises against me in judgment, god shall condemn" (Isaiah 54:17 NIV).

Sheaba watched her husband battle within himself, and she watched the devil make efforts to torture him with pain. At times Sheaba did not know how to pray, but she would touch him and pray silently whatever came up. The devil thought he was winning, but he was losing. The more he raised up in Jack, the stronger she got in recognizing his devices. She knew her husband, and he was a fighter as well. When the enemy got wind of Jack's fighting back, he would find a different way to distract him. Whenever it appeared they were on the road to recovery, the enemy would strike either one of them to start an argument. Sheaba's emotions would always flare Jack's anger and frustration, but she could not help the way she felt. Sometimes his decision making was off putting when it came to dealing with women. She felt at times she was put last and everyone else in his path was put first. It was not easy feeling alone and left out, as she wanted to return to him that same pain she was feeling. He never listened or tried to understand; and when he did, there was always a rebuttal or a better reason why he was right, and she was wrong. Sheaba's anger would always rise, and she had to remind herself that she was considered as sheep for the slaughter (Romans 8:36). It was her destiny to take on the struggles and rise above them so that her adversaries might see God within her. There was nothing she could do on her own without God to possibly turn things around for the better in her marriage or in her life. The only human thing she could do was listen for God's instructions on how to move. It was God's will for Sheaba to stop looking at Jack's flaws, and focus on herself, to allow God to assist her with making valid changes (2 Corinthians 13:5). She had to walk by faith and not by sight (2 Corinthians 5:7) and make provision to trust in the Lord with all her heart and lean not unto her own understanding but in all her ways acknowledge God, and he would direct her path. It was not wise for her to see things through her own eyes but through the eyes of God, that she might be saved from evilness. In that, God would bring health to her navel and marrow to her bones (Proverbs 3:5–8). As she accepts God's Word into her life, it would ultimately nourish her body inside out and bring fruit from out of her loins into the souls of those among her. That was Sheaba's end goal after her marriage was over. She had prayed all she could Pray for Jack. It was time to give him over to God and let him do his perfect work, because Sheaba was tired.

Sheaba thought Jack wanted the same thing God wanted for them—blissful love! But he clearly had a different agenda. His behavior did not show her love; he wanted control. He wanted things to go the way he wanted them, and it was only for his joy and not Sheaba's. Sheaba was alone for a long time; without a man, that is one that was considered to love her and cherish her the way God had. Sheaba thought, *am I supposed to be alone? But, If God desired for anyone to be alone, he would not have designed marriage. God honors marriage in that he created woman out of the rib of man, so that man would not suffer being alone. His word also said that two is better than one.* But, like Eve, Sheaba overstepped her boundaries in her marriage, having partial knowledge of her wifely behavior as a woman of God, she handed her husband a bitter, and unripe piece of fruit that rotted his heart toward her. She too played a part in Jack's behavior, but not as much as he pushed her to act out of character. God gave Sheaba a specific duty to love her husband and push through the struggles that would come, and he would take control of the rest. God showed Sheaba how much he loved Jack and was using her body to win him over. In reality, she was never supposed to marry Jack, but the connection that the two felt in the beginning superseded what God's original plan was for them. Because Sheaba missed what God was showing her, she married Jack and messed up his plan, therefore, God shifted and so did the plan.

As God continued to work on restoring her marriage, he rejuvenated her love for both him and Jack. Sheaba was already in love with God, but he wanted to give her the desires of her heart, so like Jacob went through to get his heart's desire for Rachel, so would she for Jack. Although Sheaba did not ask verbally for Jack to be returned, God heard her heart. They both wanted Jack, and what better way to get him than through Sheaba, whom he was pruning for true love.

The threefold chord of God had to be embedded in her to break through the force field of the enemy. The walls of her heart were thick and sturdy, and only the power of God could bring them down. Many months went by in Sheaba's marriage. She messed up too many times with that little member in her mouth. She regretted every moment because she received chastisement from God, and she also had to experience the feeling as if she were starting all over with the fight within her husband. The enemy laughed so hard that Sheaba could feel the frustration in the pit of her stomach, so much so that it weakened her and moved stress into her body, where she experienced a loss of energy. For a few weeks she waddled in her weakness, complained, and blamed Jack as well as other things until she received another wake-up call from God.

He reminded her that he called her to do a job, and he would not stop until it was fulfilled. The job would not only save her husband but would teach her how to sustain her marriage through godly behavior in the midst of the diverse storms of life. He spoke to her spirit saying:

> Wives, likewise, be submissive to your own husbands, that even if some do not obey the word, they, without the word, may be won by the conduct of their wives; when they observe your chaste conduct accompanied with fear. (1 Peter 3:1–2 NKJV)

Sheaba understood submission but did not know how to apply it, especially with her fight against loving despite the return of love. What hurt the most is that she could not bring herself to do what God was asking so her husband could see the God in her, which would lead Jack to fearing him. Overwhelmed with trying to please God and her husband, the devil reminded Sheaba of her suicide attempt in her first marriage. *How could I have possibly been in love with God and do something so selfish?* Sheaba thought. Sheaba realized that she was in spiritual warfare, but she could not get out of the web. The wickedness in high places had her trapped, she felt she did not have it in her to trust God enough to submit to her husband. *I cannot submit to God, how am I going to submit to my husband.* Sheaba thought. Sheaba could not see past Jack's unforgiveness and the way he treated her because of it. It repulsed her to think that Jack deserved the same opportunity she was given by God. How could God deem him to be worthy even when he was not treating her well.

But who was she to determine to whom God wanted to give opportunities? Sheaba knew it was wrong to think that way; what kind of God would he be if he picked out favorites? Sheaba hurt people before she began to serve God and understood that she was given the same opportunity as Jack. Returning her thoughts to the suicide attempt, she remembered how she begged God to let her die. But he spared her life and restored her health after much rest.

Instead of Sheaba giving in to the suicide reminder from the devil and carrying it out a second time, she rebuked the thought and made a declaration that she would always live for God. She proposed not to stoop so low as to take her life ever again, especially after God had already saved her from death so many times before. She believed he was saving her for a more prosperous and preserved life, and she wanted to experience that.

People told Sheaba that God would not ask her to do things that would cause as much grief as she was encountering. They warned her to get out of her marriage and yelled at her for staying in it. However, Sheaba held on to the belief that God would save her husband and their marriage will get better. God heard her cry and felt her struggle, and he stepped in to sustain her immediately.

> God is not a man that He shall lie, neither the son of man, that he should repent; hath he said, and shall he not do it? Or hath he spoken, and shall he not make it good? (Numbers 23:19 KJV)

Those words laid a foundation for Sheaba that could not be shaken! The Lord said Sheaba's husband would be saved; he said he would be a pillar in the kingdom of God. He asked that she show a deeper love toward Jack that he might see God's face and not hers. As Abraham was seen God through a burning bush rather than the bush itself. However, if Sheaba fails, Jack will not see God through Sheaba, and her marriage will remain hopeless.

A hopeless marriage is not what Sheaba hoped for; so, she studied to find out what would be the gift that she would receive if Jack received God as his personal savior. She wanted to know what it meant for her to love him despite his evilness toward her. Why would God have her to do that? Sheaba learned in her studies that God is the head of man, man is the head of woman, and the woman is covered by God through her husband. *Is this why God want Jack to be in his life? As he covers Jack, Jack will cover me? Hmmm... Sheaba thought. I guess he protects me, and I build him up. I like that!* Therefore, Sheaba considered that a woman's role is powerful in her husband's life; where she pray for him to keep him strong. She thought, *I am responsible for holding my husband up in prayer consistently. Because my husband has greater responsibilities, I must be the strength of his neck. When things get tough for my husband, or he becomes overwhelmed, I must be there to support him. Jack focuses on the things of God as God leads him in the direction for his family, and he is responsible for guarding me, his wife, with his life as God did for the church.*

> But I would have you know, that the head of every man is Christ; and the head of the woman is the man; and the head of Christ is God. (1 Corinthian 11:3 KJV)

> Husbands, love your wives, just as Christ love the church and gave himself up for her. (Ephesians 5:25 NIV)

> In the same way, husbands out to love their wives as their own bodies. He who loves his wife loves himself. After all, no one ever hated their own body, but they feed and care for their body, just as Christ does the church, for we are members of his body. (Ephesians 5:28-20 NIV)

> A man ought not to cover his head, since he is the image and glory of God, but woman is the glory of man. For man, does not come from woman, but woman from man; neither was man created for woman, but woman for man.

> It is for this reason that a woman ought to have authority
> over her own head, because of the angels. Nevertheless,
> in the Lord woman is not independent of man, nor is man
> independent of woman. For as the woman came from man,
> so also man is born of woman. But everything comes from
> God. (1 Corinthians 11:7–12 NIV).

Because of the chord of the Lord, man is under oath and is held responsible to guard his family with his life. He builds a hedge of protection for his family so nothing can separate them. Husbands are a creation of the face of God, that they must be esteemed, appreciated, and upheld. Wives are the epitome of God's love and must be esteemed, appreciated, and upheld. Both have distinctive roles that God has designed to be carried out to master his plan. Together with God, no guile shall overtake their marriage. God's free will brings about a balance to man and woman, in that they become one sound— the sound of love, joy, peace, and honor. Their voices are distinct, but their actions are equivalent. They harmonize in the presence of God and are synchronized with his rhythm. That is a marriage strongly tied together with the chord of the Lord! *Wow! said Sheaba. While it all sounds a bit confusing, I think I got it. Submission is hard work, but if God honors it, he will help me through it.*

The Battle between Human Love and Godly Love

Naturally, love had always filled Sheaba's belly, which made her fall hard. It took over her mind, body, and soul. Her eyes were closed off to everything but man. Sweet music played from the beat of her heart; she was excited by the touch of his hands. His voice brought melody to her ears, and her senses gave way to his emotions. Oh Yes! It caused a ruckus with every organ in her body. Her legs were debilitated, her feet were prickly, her arms were flaccid, her voice was terminated, and it threw her thoughts off track. Oh, how strong was the grip of his love! The sound of his panting overwhelmed her soul with excitement, as it confirmed his pleasure. Her eyes twinkled with passion, knowing he adored every thought of her. This man was truly a dream come true, but would he stay? Was his love truly authentic, or was it just for the moment or for a little while? What if she hit a bad nerve within him? Would he run away and never return, or would he forgive her and keep their love steady?

Spiritually, love covered her inner and outer courts. It took her mind, body, and soul by surprise and shocked them. It caused her eyes to be opened to avenues beyond her understanding. It invited the brightest light that exposed her being. As it made its way inside of her, it searched her, proved her, imparted and seasoned her. While her body gave way to the sweet sensation, it trembled, and his voice comforted her soul. He spoke sweet nothings in her ear, the kind that no man could ever utter without a touch. Her lips touched his lips and were filled with the fruit of his love. As she yielded her tongue to him, it waxed numb, and a new language of love rolled off it. Their hands joined, and her life was synergized with his life. Her feet were like rabbit feet as they hastily moved to connect with him. The passion was overwhelmingly strong, and her heart skipped several beats. Tears flowed rapidly down her face. Her mouth hung wide open, trying to belt out the joy of the moment. The climax of his presence relaxed her, and his soft touch gave her rest. Oh, how could it be that her heart was captured without charm. With just one touch, he made her whole again. He held her, encouraged her, and loved her when she made him angry and when she made him happy. What manner of man was this, that he would love her despite her faults? He was a dream come true and one that would never leave her side.

There was no doubt that both forms of love felt extremely good. The question was, which one was true and everlasting? Sheaba's love toward her husband was authentic in her own way, but God's way would have prevented the evil alterations that tore her marriage apart. She learned through the chord of the Lord that circumstantial love is not of God, but a love that binds creates a foundation from God that cannot be shaken. Agape love opens the eyes of the blind, while circumstantial love blinds. Sheaba and Jack tormented themselves as they opened the door to circumstantial love. They depended on each other to do what they desired in their flesh, rather than the things God had already set in place for them. Although Sheaba had been serving God for some time, she had no clue how to love the way God loved her because humanity only understand mutual love versus sacrificial love.

The two had nothing in common; they were, in the natural, forbidden to be together, yet it was God who pricked both their spirits and allowed the forbidden in the natural. Neither Jack nor Sheaba understood what they were feeling or what was happening, but Sheaba always felt her spirit man's joy when she thought of Jack. Both Sheaba and Jack shared those same emotions on the day of their marriage, and experienced the greatest peace, as well as the stillness of time. That day felt like a miracle from God. It welcomed a respect, a peace, a connection that humans are unable to identify with because it is unnatural to them to love that way. However, that love only lasted for such a short period of time. They had two different motives for the direction of the marriage, and they began to bump heads quickly.

Unfortunately, in a twinkle of an eye, Sheaba's marriage was over. The emotional and mental abuse was overwhelming and Sheaba's mind was about to pop. To stay in the marriage would have been death to the birth of new life in Jack, because Sheaba would have demolished every inch of his manhood with her aggression. Sheaba wanted to keep her integrity and good character in tact; defiling her mouth and her temple would have been death to her spiritual baby; yet again. If that would have happened a second time, Sheaba may not have had the opportunity to become impregnated with the gift of God's ministry ever again. It was Sheaba's belief that she would return to living her secular life and relieve herself of spirituality for good.

Sheaba's carnal mind prevented her from obtaining the true knowledge of the wars and fightings that lived within. When she released her mind to the wisdom of God she was able to recognize the fight inside that murdered a Godly kind of love. Sheaba thought, *as I have come through the womb of flesh, I have inherited the sins that lived inside the one that carried me. Therefore, I was nourished with societal views long before I understood what life was about.* Sheaba reminded herself of the thought daily by reading the book of Psalms 51, as she learned how she must allow God to live inside in order to receive his nourishment of wisdom and knowledge.

> For I was born a sinner, yes, from the moment my mother conceived me. But you desired honesty from the womb, teaching me wisdom even there. (Psalm 51:5–6 NLT)

Reading Psalm 121 brought on a day of reckoning for Sheaba, look to the heavens from where your help comes from. The heaviness that laid upon her heart regarding true loving relationships interrupted her vision of relationships; the exposure of emotional abuse irregulated her heartbeat. Sheaba was in a bad marriage and had been blinded to the truth of her and Jack. Both Jack and Sheaba were dysfunctional; they had never experienced true love, but believed they had. Growing up they lacked love and attention from family, and they were not connected to the love of God. Having the love of God inside would have replaced the enraged, aggressive, and empty spaces they possessed. To share with people what was happening in their marriage would have brought natural attacks rather than spiritual guidance. Therefore, Sheaba refrained from sharing because she did not want to hinder their optimistic view of her marriage; she turned to the bible to see what the Lord had to say as she prayed:

> I lift up my eyes to the mountains; where does my help come from? My help comes from the Lord, the Maker of heaven and earth. He will not let your foot slip, he who watches over you will not slumber. Indeed, he that watches over Israel will neither slumber nor sleep. The Lord watches over you, the Lord is your shade at your right hand, the sun will not harm you by day, nor the moon by night. The Lord will keep you from all harm, he will watch over your life. The Lord will watch over your coming and going both now and forever more. (Psalm 121 NIV)

Sheaba learned that the world would side with her on the natural outlook of situations because the world says it is unorthodox and unethical. But God is unorthodox. He will use things that are abnormal to confound the minds of humans.

> But to those whom God has called, both Jews and Greeks, Christ the power of God and the wisdom of God. For the foolishness of God is wiser than human wisdom, and the weakness of God is stronger than human strength. Brothers and sisters think of what you were when you were called. Not many of you were wise by human standards; not many were influential; not many were of noble birth. But God chose the foolish things of the world to shame the wise; God chose the weak things of the world to shame the strong. God chose the lowly things of this world and the despised things and the things that are not to nullify the things that are, so that no one may boast before him. It is because of him that you are in Christ Jesus, who has become from God that is, our righteousness, holiness, and redemption. Therefore, as it is written: "Let the one who boasts boast in the Lord." (1 Corinthians 1:24–31 NIV)

Sheaba realized the scripture was factual and a good example of what God expected from her. Just as his son Jesus loved the world and it did not love him back, so was Sheaba to love her husband even though he did not show love toward her. It was her assignment; although it was tough in her flesh, she pressed through it in the spirit. God had given her many signs that Jack was not chosen for her covering, but she missed every one of them, so she had to go through the struggles and complete the assignment by faith. Society can not relate with that theology, but Sheaba had no choice but to take a shot at it; she had already married the man. Sheaba believed God had a plan and thought maybe he wanted her and Jack to see their situation with hopeful eyes. He used the things that appeared hurtful and immoral to Sheaba's flesh to strengthen her in him (God), not to demoralize or bring harm. It was when she could rid the visions of the natural and fight with the Word of God, that her marriage appeared to be at peace. It stopped the enemy's plight for her to fight with Jack. God knew she would get it right, so he gave her a second chance at her marriage.

When God rekindled Sheaba and Jack marriage one year after the divorce, they experienced almost their entire first year of the same turmoil. Then God stepped in, grabbed Sheaba's spirit man, guided her the remainder of the way with his words of wisdom and knowledge. It was hard to grab hold of God's chord of love again, as the flesh only believed what the world showed her about love—that was all she knew, even in her walk with God. But God showed her the opposite of what her flesh could relate to and led her in a direction of the reality of life. Sheaba and Jack were fed through the chord of the Lord and returned to their journey, not only as husband and wife but as a man and a woman of God. Yet, it was still hard because they had to be taught how to apply the true effects of love to their life and to each other. Agape (Selfless/Spirit) love was at war with Ludas (Playful/Emotion) love, so, they continued to battle in their marriage, and the ending was more brutal that time than the first.

I Surrender; I Say Yes to Your Will

Before Sheaba could receive the total understanding of the chord of the Lord, she had to surrender (give up completely) her life truly to God. Without doing that, she would consistently be bound to areas of her flesh pulling her in diverse directions. In surrendering to Christ, not only did she expect to get her husband back, but her divine site and joy. Sheaba's relationship with God had gotten stronger, she was able to articulate relational situations beyond her natural understanding. However, she was not to get out of her marriage regardless of what God had shown her, unless Jack was ready to bail out. Sometimes that disappointed Sheaba, as she had grown weary with him. So, she allowed God to give her wisdom on how to deal with it. She knew God was not blaming her for how she viewed herself and the relationships she engaged, nor for the situations that occurred in her marriage. It felt like a lesson that had to be learned for her lack obedience.

Sheaba believed she was the epitome of love because even though people did things rudely to her, she would forgive them and treat them as if they had done nothing afterward. Though she thought she knew how to love like Christ, it was typically a hard pill to swallow and difficult to apply his kind of love to her own life. God is omniscient (all knowing), he was aware that Sheaba was not wise in the knowledge and understanding of his true agape love because her marriage consistently failed in that area. So, God waited for her to surrender that area of her life to him so he could show her the depth of his love and how to apply it. Now Sheaba had made countless efforts to apologize to Jack, even when she believed she was not completely wrong or wrong at all. She held herself accountable for what she believed God instructed her to do when she was attacked with offence and other evil tactics.

Sheaba did not forget her disobedience. She sought God to continue to teach of her wrong. This is what she learned about what happens in obedience: As she surrendered to the will of God, her repentance opened her heart and soul to his voice. God showed her the pain and the joy of relationship and how they both could be positive if she allowed him to reside between them. Pain in the flesh is the price paid to have true joy. As the flesh dies to its lusts, the spirit unleashes a positivity that spreads throughout the body quicker than the spread of a disease. A *yes* rose up in Sheaba's spirit as she was receiving the acknowledgement of obedience through prayer, which allowed God to cleanse her of the infection she had created within. Her *yes* created a sacrifice to accept whatever God would take her through and always serve him, no matter what. That *yes* sacrifice showed her in a vision, things that normally overwhelmed her flesh and would cause it to disobey the instructions of God. But her yes would override it and bring strength. Her yes reminded her that love (Jesus) died on the cross so that sinners like her could live. Love was beaten, spat on, kicked, and pierced to prove his love to the world. Love endured the pain and left his instructions to teach the world how to overcome it. Love purchased her and made her to be enslaved to him on all points of life, with no exceptions.

Loving her husband in the spiritual way was the hardest thing to do. She assumed she was a pro at loving others, but God proved her wrong. Sheaba wanted to be given something she was not giving, and God was not allowing it. Sheaba believed it was too late because in her efforts to show Godly love to Jack, he was already numb from all the calamity that had occurred between them previously. He had enough of the constant discomfort and disappointments. He had enough of the inconsistency. He did not have it in him to return the affection to Sheaba that she began to give him. Jack said it did not feel real to him.

Although he said he loved her dearly, she did not believe him either. Her natural abilities murdered every attempt to pour out spiritual love. The connection they once shared began to die along with the desire to remain together. Sheaba still did not give up; she continued to do as God instructed—to show love through affection, regardless of the circumstance, and to be happy while doing it. In doing so, she finally experienced the difference of natural and spiritual love in her bones. It felt good to love Jack past the pain. Every morning when she got up and again before going to bed, she looked forward to thrusting love upon Jack. Unfortunately, after growing weary of not receiving the love in return, she stepped out of the alignment of God again and allowed flesh to be resuscitated, and love was shifted both naturally and spiritually. Sheaba's yes had become a no, and the will of God was hindered in maintaining and strengthening her marriage, even though it thrived in gaining a soul.

It did not stop there. God proved to both Sheaba and Jack that without him, their minds would be continuously enslaved by diverse evil contentions. They would always be at odds and never be able to rekindle the love that he poured into them. Both were joined in the *no* concept, and divorce infiltrated their hearts, which started a sore on the inside and forced its way out. Hatred infected their souls and broke every strand of love that God taught them. Sheaba knew that to give in to God was to live a prominent life, while Jack had an idea but needed her to exemplify a godly wife to push him. He needed her help, and God knew it, which is why he allowed them to be joined together in the first place. Their lack of understanding, as well as their reluctance to say yes to the will of God, was burying their marriage in the ground.

God had another plan that neither of them saw coming. He was not done with them yet. Although they were mentally divorced, God breathed reconciliation in them. He dug up what was not deeply buried and formulated it in a way that it would not become irrevocably broken but resolved and dissolved; they divorced peacefully.

Reconciliation to Near Death

One year later, Jack reached out to her with a plan. Sheaba had never stopped loving Jack, but she could not see herself returning to him. As far as she knew, Jack had never stepped outside of the marriage, but she speculated that he had, and she hated his love to debate with her about almost everything. Peace and forgiveness was a bad word when she was married to him, and she refused to let him back in her life. Jack despised her because he said she whine too much and was always accusing him of cheating. Most of all, her lack of trust sickened him. Sheaba scarred his ego with hurtful words when she felt he was pounding her ego and felt no remorse.

Unknowingly, through Jack's consistency in attending church services and bible studies, he began to say yes in his spirit. He was first convicted for following through with the first divorce, and then disobedience toward God. Jack started calling Sheaba a lot and having discussions about the bible. Sheaba recorded every call as Jack had a habit of saying she said things she did not say. Whenever he got obnoxiously demonstrative, she would remind him that she did not have to answer his calls if he continued that attitude. Jack apologized, but Sheaba warned him that she was not going to have any conversations about his and her pass marriage, but she was open to talking about God and other things.

Jack expressed how much he wanted to be married again, "my next wife will become one with me on the top of a mountain unclothed." "I believe the love connection their will began a marriage that has a great bond of love." Sheaba expressed immediately, "I wish you the best! I am definitely not interested in us reconciling. I am happy with where I am today." Jack responded, "in my mind divorcing you was wrong, but all I could think of was I could not get that love we had in the beginning to return." Sheaba said, ok thank you, now can we change the subject?" "I would like to meet someone who conveyed the love we had in the beginning; I know God desires that I have a spiritual woman." Sheaba ended the call as she was disappointed with his conversation and felt it was not something she wanted to discuss at that moment.

The more Jack called and talked about God, the more Sheaba realized he was actually trying to see if she was still interested in him. Sheaba messed up when she allowed him to know that she had not been in a relationship the entire time they were divorced. Jack found every angle to fit her into his life indirectly. He began to tell her, "I have been fasting and praying and God has been really blessing me. Every time I ask him for something, he gives it to me and so I must be careful of what I ask of him. I have been praying for a wife, and I believe he will give her to me by the end of this year. I love the fall months and enjoy watching sports with her and movies." Sheaba already knew what he loved and was trying to understand why he thought she should know what he was after.

Jack strengthened himself mentally and physically to work with Sheaba in a way that compromised her thoughts toward him. Sheaba loved Jack still but did not trust him; he had always had an agenda. His subtle pursuit alarmed her and sent her back to their past. She could not let go of her past thoughts of Jack long enough to see if it were God or the enemy working on him and through him. As Jack made greater efforts to appeal to her emotions through consistently driving his apologetics of their past and present marriage, Sheaba shot them down. She did it as respectful and as nice as she could. She respected what he was trying to do, but saying it was not enough to rekindle their vows.

Jack still did not give up. At times he would throw cheese for her to bite, but she was too smart for that. The feelings inside were strong for him, but she did not want him to know how she truly felt. She never wanted the divorce, and always tried to get Jack to work on their differences, but he was too unforgiving and angry. It was then that Sheaba decided to give him his heart's desire.

Sheaba was still married to Jack emotionally but physically divorced, however, she had become selfish in sharing the love she received from God with Jack. The thought of giving that up to reconnect with Jack, was preposterous. But Jack continued to pursue Sheaba until she gave in to him. Fortunately, her heart began to turn with Jack's last attempt. He proposed another conversation but this time with her Pastor and his wife (Pastor and Co-Pastor Bradford). Sheaba still being stubborn, did not feel the attraction and tried again to turn Jack down. She realized the look in his eyes at that moment was sincere disappointment. He left the counseling session without Sheaba and with hurt feelings. Nothing more came out of his mouth that day to her and he would not even look in her direction. Sheaba did not want to care but she did; she felt bad. but could not allow her heart to give him what he wanted—at least she thought she knew what he wanted. Before he left Sheaba tried giving him a hug, but he barely received it. Sheaba refused to take it personally but smiled at him and thanked him for his efforts.

Sheaba thought about what had taken place for a few days and then released it to God. A part of her was happy she did not give in, but her heart bled for him in the other part.

Just when she accepted that it was over, and they would finally be completely done with each other, Jack reached out to her without any effort at all, but with a greater love approach, one that Sheaba could not allow to pass her by. Again, after looking deeper into his eyes, and hearing his voice, which was happy, content, and confident, her heart melted. God convicted her as she was overlooking his plan. Immediately, Sheaba grabbed Jacks hands, sat him down and explained to him what she was feeling and thinking, and followed up with an apology. Jack understood; he did not expect her to take the bait of his efforts to talk with her and her leaders, but he felt he was pressed by God to continue pursuing her. After that day, time went by quickly, and before she knew it, they were celebrating his birthday. The went to a nice restaurant, they sat, ate, and talked about every issue that had harmed their marriage. The attraction between them was like bees to honey, but they contained themselves very well; cuddling was as far as it went.

Amazingly, Jack spoke a lot about God and proved to be in tune and in touch with him. Sheaba noticed some things had not changed, but she knew she could not have it all, and neither did she totally change. Not everything had come out that needed to be exposed and murdered within them, but again their dysfunctional love pulled them back together. God never allowed Sheaba and Jack to be remarried but again, Sheaba was blinded and deaf to the heeding of God's warnings. Sheaba was reminded of the pain and suffering of their past ignorance. Sheaba promised that she would enter into the second marriage with humility, love, and submission. She went in desiring better than the first.

Remembering the story in the Holy Bible's book of Hosea, primarily the pain Hosea went through and the struggles his wife, Gomer, faced. Hosea was an obedient servant of the Lord who married Gomer, a harlot. Though his heart was consistently in agony because she had run off into the streets after her lovers, he sought after her and continued to love her as his wife. Gomer could not shake her past, as it was her comfort zone. Being married to many men was what she was used to. For Gomer, Hosea put her in a prison that forced her to experience true love. Love was not real in Gomer's heart. Life was a day-by-day mishap that thrust her into a world of mess and fictitious pleasures. How could she appreciate the love and affection that her husband gave when it was unfamiliar? Pain was her attraction, and even though it was treacherous and malicious, it was her home. God ordained Hosea and Gomer's marriage for his glory; he had a purpose he wanted to display. Hosea would love a woman who rebelled against him, as Israel did against God. He would understand how God loved him and that he would never leave him, despite his sinfulness.

Therefore, God ordered Hosea to love his wife regardless of the circumstances. In the third chapter of Hosea, God reconciled the marriage of Hosea and Gomer, and there were no more episodes of Gomer running away. In Hosea's last pursuit of Gomer, he paid his dues and carried her home. In route, he communicated his commandments to her and declared he would follow them as well. His voice brought security to her soul and reached a height that propagated loyalty and love to her husband. Sheaba's thoughts of this depiction forced her to believe that she was to give in to the pursuit of Jack and submit to him the way he wanted her to do in the first marriage with no resistance. It is not understood how she got that out of that story, but she held on to it and did her best to keep Jack happy.

When the chord of the Lord is yoked about marriage, there is no way either person can run without being pulled back. Gomer was lost in a world outside of the realm of Christ. The world handed her an eros love that distorted her name, yet God pulled her into his presence to win her soul, as well as to educate Hosea. The battle between natural and spiritual love was evident in the relationship of Hosea and Gomer. Gomer loved the world, and Hosea loved God. The battle caused a pain in both of them, which must have been unbelievably difficult. However, spiritual love (Agape) dominated, as it was the most powerful.

Though spiritual love takes you through countless tough journeys, God only allows a level of pain that is tolerable. Natural love leads the soul to a black hole, where pain is inevitable, and introduces detestation. The combination of both natural and spiritual love brings about a balance, but spiritual love will always supersede all things, Sheaba thought.

Unfortunately, Sheaba was the only one with the mind to press forward past the ugly events of the first marriage. Her plan was put to a halt when after the first three months Jack purposefully showed acts of the past by entertaining phone calls from his past relations. Sheaba warned that she would not allow disrespect and would end the marriage immediately with an annulment if he did not stop. Jack said nothing as they were inside of the church talking; no one was there but them, but he determined it to be the wrong place to have that discussion. Sheaba was over the top angry and said a few choice words that laid dormant deep in her soul to Jack once they had gotten home. She was so angry that she attempted to hit him with a cast iron skillet but stopped herself; grease from the skillet splattered upside the wall. When Sheaba finally calmed down, she told Jack she knew the marriage was over already because he never forgives. Jack said nothing and did exactly what Sheaba said he was going to do.

Jack continued his plight to make Sheaba feel the pain of being alone in the marriage, so Sheaba decided to plan on moving out. It was then that Sheaba expressed to Jack that she knew he and his tenant was planning to be married before he pursued her again. He tried to deny it, but then decided to tell her that it was not her business and he did not owe her that information; but the woman still lived in the building and a week prior to the altercation they were just in, he asked her to take a package to the tenant and it was then Sheaba apologized for accusing her and Jack. Sheaba was humiliated and all the pain she felt after finding out that her accusations were true from the first marriage unleashed on him at that moment.

Jack talked Sheaba out of moving, however, the madness did not end. Jack had an exit plan; he had always warned Sheaba that he had a way to get out of anything he did not want to be a part of. Jack had five baby mothers and he was still in love with the last one who happened to be Jamaican. She lived in New York with his two youngest children. He had a daughter that lived with them, but she was all grown up with a baby. In his fear of being alone, he forced his way into the Jamaican mother's life to get her to allow him to raise the two in Champaign. The woman at one point did not know that he was married because he told Sheaba that it needed to be a secret until he get the two children. Somehow the woman found out and Jack was disappointed with Sheaba and blamed her for the exposure.

Sheaba said nothing but ignored the accusation. Shortly, thereafter, on Sheaba's birthday, Jack and the woman was on the phone planning his trip alone to New York. He had the call on speaker so Sheaba could hear the conversation. They were planning to spend a week together at her home. Sheaba and Jack had already had a conversation prior, informing him of the disrespect to the marriage. Jack wanted Sheaba's approval, but she would never talk about it anymore. She knew Jack wanted to argue and fight to make him feel comfortable about cheating.

Sheaba left and went to Alabama earlier that month and Jack used that time to accuse her of cheating on him. He had no grounds to clarify his accusation, but it was enough for him to justify his trip. Sheaba said to him, "I am glad you feel that way, with all the things you have done against the marriage, you should feel uncomfortable." Sheaba knew that he had a made-up mind already but wanted an excuse to do his dirt. Sheaba feeling jilted and hurt behind what he was doing picked up Jack's already made drink when he left the room and drank it instead of praying as she normally would do. That was the worst thing she could have done. Whatever was in his drink made her sick and impaired her vision; she was drugged and out of her mind. Nothing was clear from that point on. Everything that happened was in sections; one while she understood what was going on and the next moment she did not.

The last thing Sheaba remembered was Jack doing something to her and laughing when she was trying to get into the bed. Sheaba remembered taking a pillow and throwing it at him and then she found herself swinging and backing up; but everything was pitch black. It felt like she was fighting an invisible person in darkness. She then felt her body being gripped like a glove and was lifted off her feet. Jack's voice then was heard in the silence, "you know I am about to call the police!" He said it three times while spitting in her face; she had no idea it was blood until later. Sheaba passed out, she was not sure how long, but when she had awakened, everything was still pitch black. It must have been the pain; Sheaba gasped for air as she recognized Jack's knee in her neck and the other on her left leg.

As she tried to scream out to let him know she could not breathe, he yelled at her to shut up while applying more pressure. Sheaba lifted her right hand to tap him and he bit her fingers, pulled them apart so as to break them and pulled her wedding ring he gave her off her finger. Before Sheaba passed out again, she heard Jack screaming to his daughter to call the police as if he were in distress.

As Sheaba began to awaken again, she still could not see, but could hear the police radios. She heard them asking her to get up, but her limbs would not obey her mind. Still unsure of how she had gotten off the floor, she realized there were a room full of cops, Jack's daughter, and her boyfriend, and she was naked underneath a robe that was not intact. Someone helped her put on some pants, but the cops did not allow her to put anything else on. They took her to the hospital, where she was told by the nurse that they were not going to check her entire body after she explained her head, throat, fingers, and legs were in excruciating pain. The nurse only wrapped her leg after explaining it was broken and then the police hauled her to jail. Sheaba stayed there for 3 days and 2 nights waiting to see the judge to be released.

Sheaba fought to win the case against Jack, but the law in Champaign stated, the first person to call the police was the victim. The pictures of Sheaba's swollen face, bruised fingers, bruised hip, and broken leg was not enough to win; the judge ruled in Jack's favor because she said Sheaba hit Jack first and she admitted it, regardless of her state of incoherence. Sheaba served one year of probation, supervision, restitution, and counseling, along with a protection order against her by Jack. Sheaba was now a criminal who had a Domestic Battery case attached to her name. Her integrity and character as a woman of God was compromised, all because she missed the warnings of God.

Sheaba had learned of her selfishness from the time she was a toddler; her anger and aggression from the time she was a young child; and her promiscuity, anger, and aggression as a teenager to an adult. It was a war that almost ruined her life. It was not easy to understand that the war in her members would destroy her until she gained the wisdom of God. If she had not developed the *'yes''* concept to embrace God and take him at his word, she would have drowned in her sorrows and died in her sins. Wisdom showed her where she was wrong in areas where she thought she was right inside and outside of her marriage. It opened her eyes to a new life that predicted a future that she could only hope that her faith in God would provide favor.

Sheaba knew she was not the only one who experienced war before wisdom; everyone has at some point in their lives. Sheaba, however, made a valid decision and a strong effort to recognize she needed help, and she sought God for it. In her mind she thought it was a bit foolish to listen to an invisible being and follow his instructions, but she continued to believe, and the result of it took her on a ride that led her through Damascus to the Promised Land. Saying "yes" and surrendering to God's will paid off! However, the war was so great that she almost lost her life, but the wisdom of God thrusted her body into the heavenlies that rejected her demise.

There is still war in the members of her body, but the wisdom of God moved in such a way that caused her to see him in the midst of war, which evicted the raging storms of life. Her life was changed thereafter because she later understood there was always war before wisdom.

Printed in the United States
By Bookmasters